Atticus Greene Haygood

Pure songs for Sunday-schools

Atticus Greene Haygood

Pure songs for Sunday-schools

ISBN/EAN: 9783337266356

Printed in Europe, USA, Canada, Australia, Japan

Cover: Foto ©Thomas Meinert / pixelio.de

More available books at **www.hansebooks.com**

PURE SONGS

FOR

SUNDAY-SCHOOLS.

EDITED BY

REV. ATTICUS G. HAYGOOD, D.D.,

AND

R. M. McINTOSH.

MACON, GA.:
PUBLISHED BY J. W. BURKE & CO.
SOUTHERN METHODIST PUBLISHING HOUSE, NASHVILLE, TENN.
ADVOCATE PUBLISHING CO., ST. LOUIS, MO.

[COPYRIGHT, 1889, BY J. W. BURKE & CO.]

PREFACE.

PURE SONGS differs from all other books of its class, with which we are acquainted, in two essential particulars:

1. It abounds with songs founded on the parables, miracles, and leading texts and incidents of the Holy Scriptures, making it easy to illustrate and emphasize Bible instruction with song. This feature, so far as we know, is new, and we expect the best results to follow from its introduction. The mere statement of such a plan is sufficient, we think, to impress all intelligent people with its importance, argument being unnecessary.

2. PURE SONGS contains an unusual number of the better forms of Church tunes, adapted to hymns in general use. If this department of the book is utilized by those who have charge of music in the Sunday-School, the effect will soon be perceptible in the improvement of congregational singing among our Churches.

Believing that our people need such a book, we send them " PURE SONGS " hoping that, under God's blessing, it may aid them in their work, and be productive of much good.

THE EDITORS.

Emory College, Oxford, Ga.,
June, 1889.

PURE SONGS.

No. 1. JESUS IS MINE.

R. M. McIntosh, by per.

1 Fade, fade each earthly joy, Je - sus is mine; Break ev-'ry ten-der tie,
2 Tempt not my soul a - way, Je - sus is mine; Here would I ev - er stay,
3 Farewell, ye dreams of night, Je - sus is mine; Lost in this dawning light,
4 Farewell, mor - tal - i - ty, Je - sus is mine; Welcome e - ter - ni - ty,

Je - sus is mine; Dark is the wil - der-ness, Earth has no
Je - sus is mine; Per - ish - ing things of clay, Born but for
Je - sus is mine; All that my soul has tried, Left but a
Je - sus is mine; Wel-come, O loved and blest, Welcome, sweet

rest - ing place, Je - sus a - lone can bless, Je - sus is mine.
one brief day, Pass from my heart a - way, Je - sus is mine.
dis - mal void,—Je - sus has sat - is - fied, Je - sus is mine.
scenes of rest, Wel-come my Saviour's breast, Je - sus is mine.

No. 3. HALLELUJAH! BLESS HIS NAME!

J. H. K.   J. H. KURZENKNABE.

1 A sin-ner, I came, for my Lord to see, Hal-le - lu - jah, bless his name!
2 I knew that the Lord would not pass me by, Hal-le - lu - jah, bless his name!
3 Oh, the rapture I felt I can nev - er tell, Hal-le - lu - jah, bless his name!
4 I'll watch, for to-day yet the Lord may come, Hal-le - lu - jah, bless his name!

He knew me at once and a-bode with me, Hal-le - lu - jah, bless his name!
He knows ev-'ry heart, and he heard my cry, Hal-le - lu - jah, bless his name!
For the great relief when my burden fell, Hal-le - lu - jah, bless his name!
To grant me the joy of his happy home, Hal-le - lu - jah, bless his name!

CHORUS.

Hal-le - lu - jah, oh, the glo - ry! Je-sus loves me, this I know;
Hal-le-lu-jah!
For I feel the bless - ed par - don That our Sav-iour did be - stow.

Copyrighted, 1886, by J. H. Kurzenknabe.

No. 6. THE LAMB OF CALVARY.

Rev. J. H. Martin, D. D. R. M. McIntosh.

1 There was love, deep love, in the cross dis-played, When the Lamb of Cal-va-ry died, For the slaves of sin was a ran-som paid, When the Lamb of Cal-va-ry died.
2 There is love, strong love, in the King on high To the souls condemned for their guilt, He will save the lost that to him draw nigh Thro' the pre-cious blood that he spilt.
3 There is love, warm love, in the Sav-iour's heart For the troub-led, wretched, and weak; In his bound-less grace he will peace im-part To the mourn-er, low-ly and meek.
4 Un-to Je-sus come with your load of grief, And re-pose by faith on his breast, There your bur-dened spir-it shall find re-lief— On the Lamb of Cal-va-ry rest.

REFRAIN.

'Twas a bless-ed, bless-ed day for our wretch-ed race

Copyright, 1885, by R. M. McIntosh.

THE LAMB OF CALVARY. Concluded.

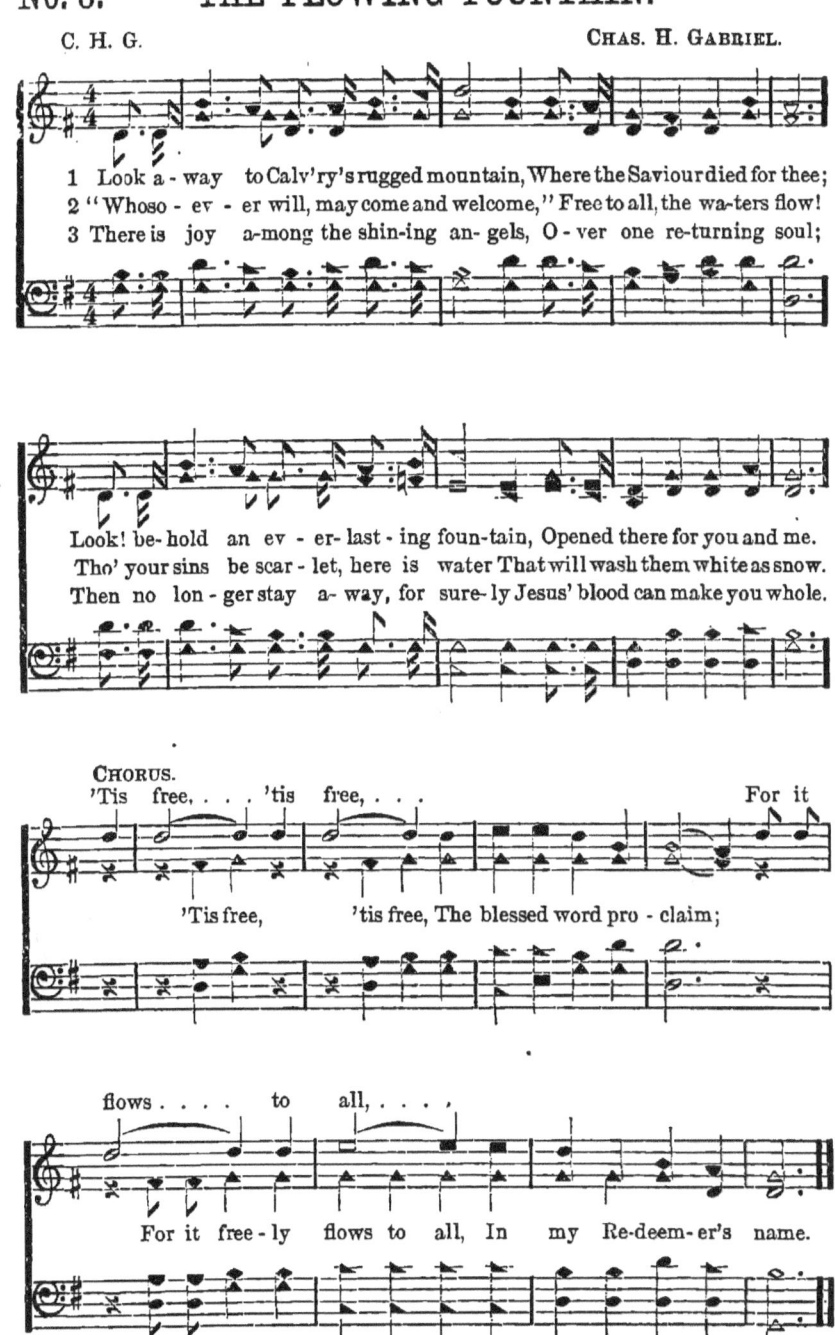

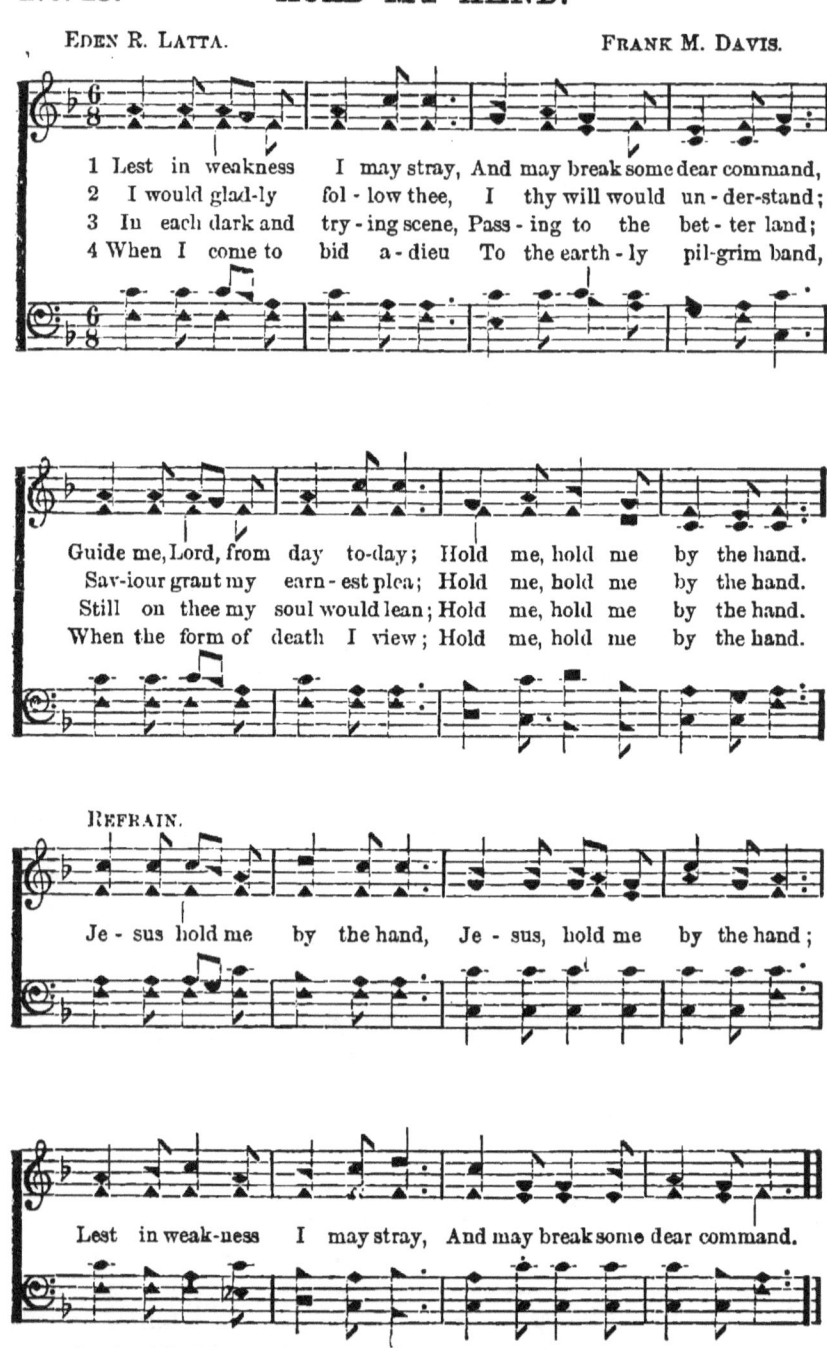

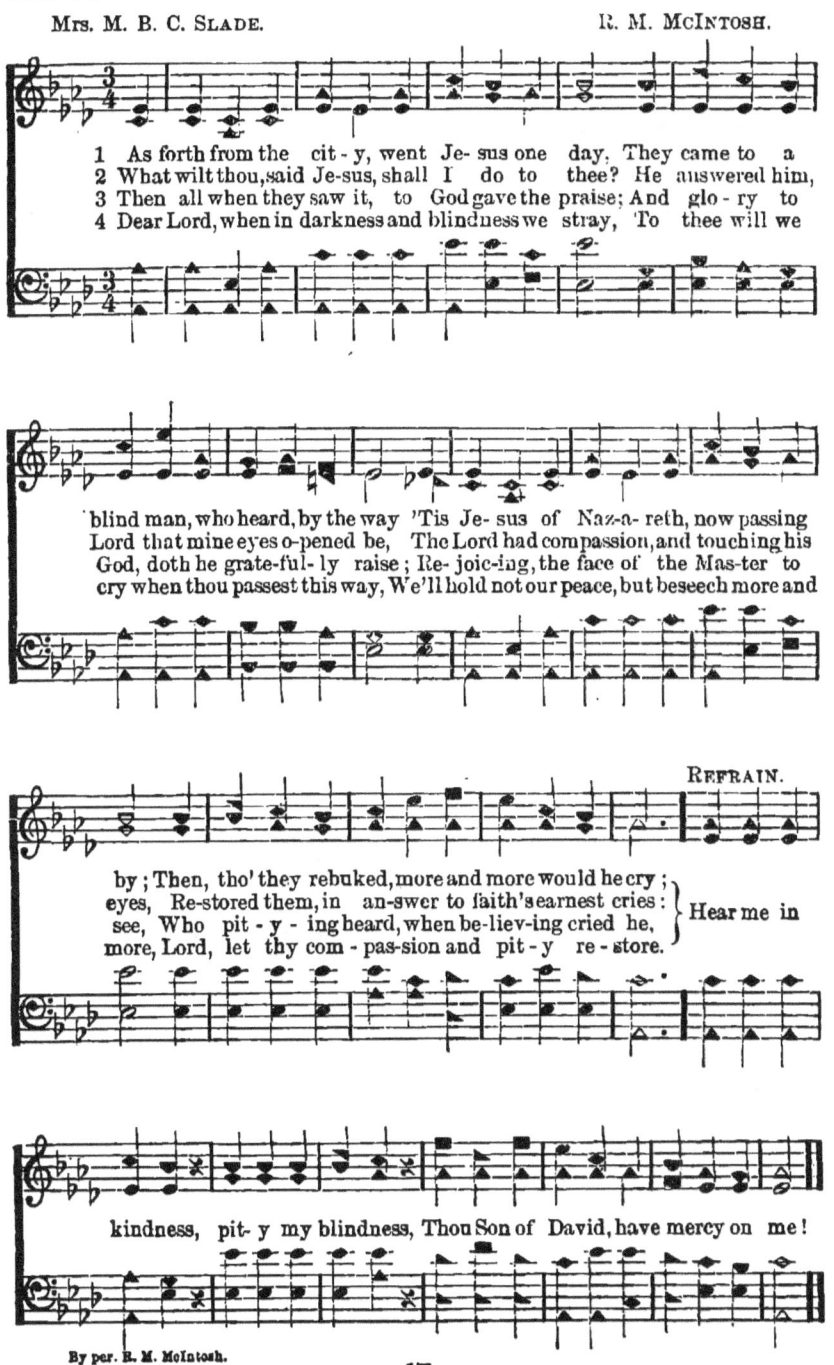

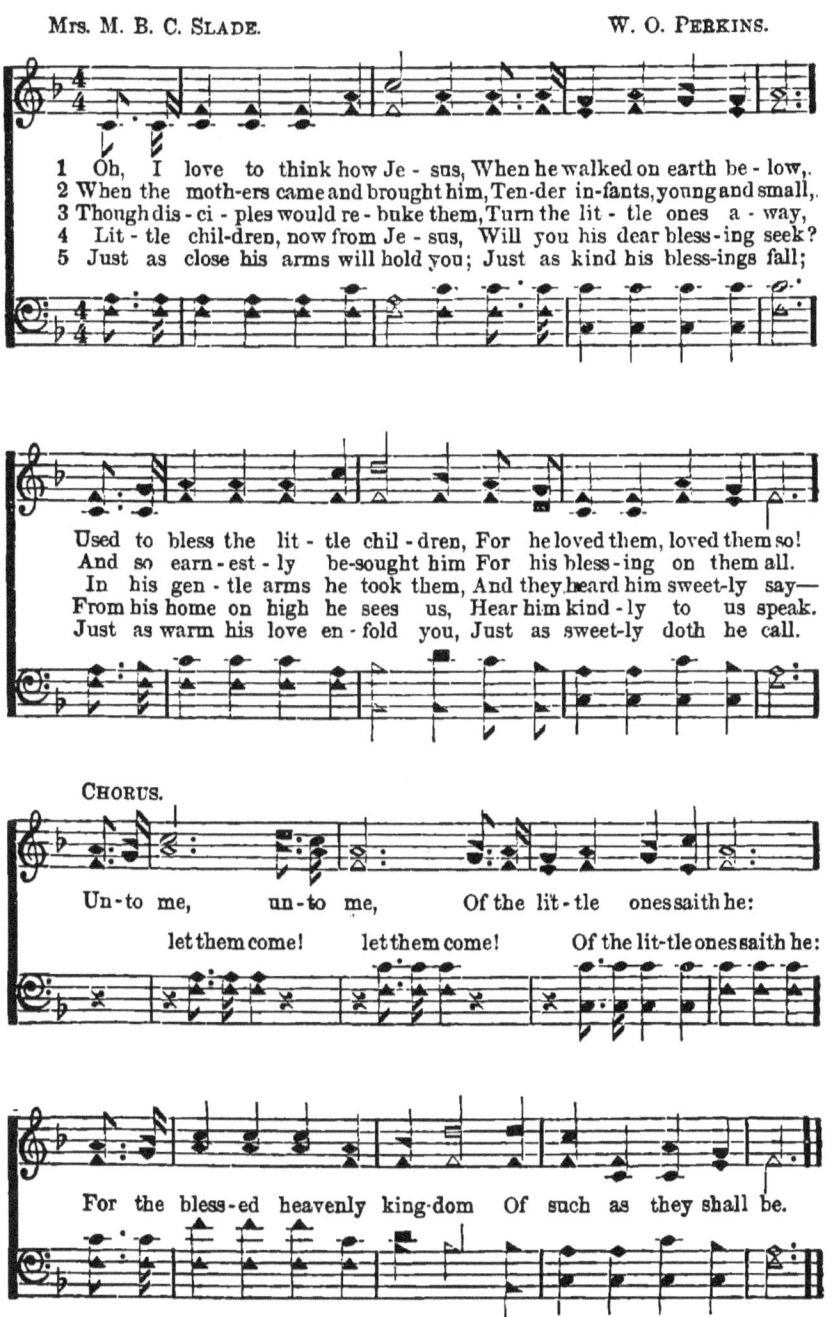

No. 17. THE SINLESS SUMMERLAND.

Arranged from J. W. WELSH.   J. C. BUSHEY.

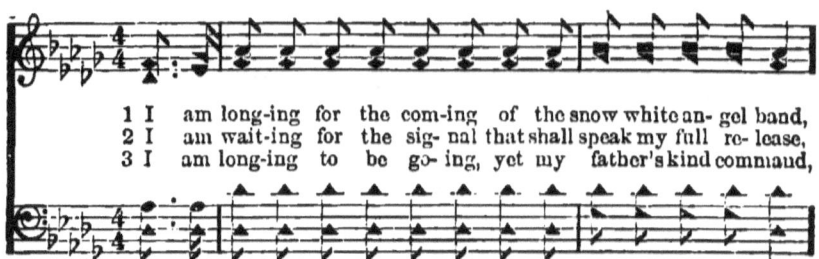

1 I am long-ing for the com-ing of the snow white an- gel band,
2 I am wait-ing for the sig- nal that shall speak my full re- lease,
3 I am long-ing to be go- ing, yet my father's kind command,

That shall bear my wea- ry spir - it, To the sin-less sum-mer-land,
And pre - sent my welcome passport, To the realms of per- fect peace,
Bid's me tar - ry 'mid the shadows Of the mist- y low - er - land,

As I tread the nar-row pathway, Thro' this thorn-y vale I dream
Yes, and when the wea- ry san- dals All the dust - y way have trod,
When my pil- grim-age is end - ed, I shall stem the tur - bid flood,

Of the joys that ev - er brighten, Where the pear- ly wa- ters gleam.
I shall sing a-mong the an- gels By the gold- en throne of God.
And re - cline up- on the bos-om, Of the spot-less Son of God.

Copyright, 1885, by R. M. McIntosh.

THE SINLESS SUMMERLAND. Concluded.

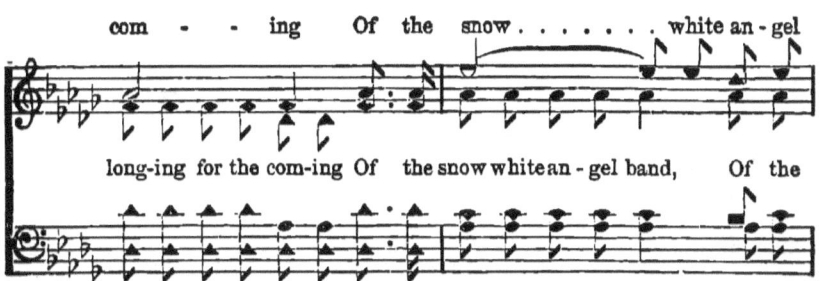

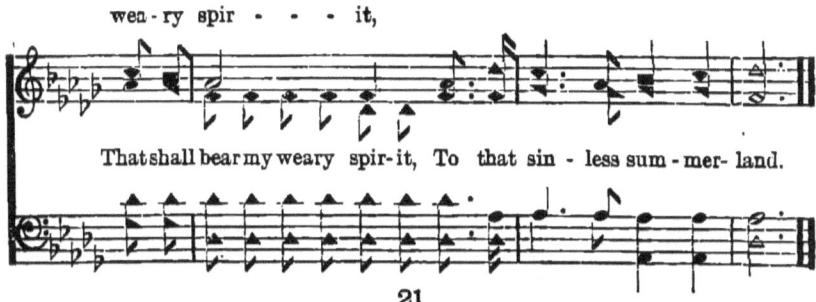

No. 19. THE MUSTARD SEED.

Mrs. M. B. C. Slade. R. M. McIntosh.

1 Lik - en the kingdom to the springing, Springing of smallest seeds we know:
2 Say not, too humble seems thy planting, Trust in the sto - ry Je - sus told,
3 O! the re-joic-ing, when at e - ven, Thy la - bor end - ed, safe at home,

Soon in the branches birds are singing, So shall the heav'nly kingdom grow.
Dews of his grace our Lord is grant-ing, Soon shall it yield an hundred fold.
High in the branches, up in heaven, Singing, "O! Lord thy kingdom's come!"

CHORUS.

Wide o'er the mead, Fling thou the seed! Sun - shine of heav - en shall be giv - en; Seed of the king - dom free - ly sow.

By per. R. M. McIntosh.

Would you go Home with the Angels. Concluded.

Ask him in faith, Je-sus will save; His life for you he gave.

No. 21.   HARP. C. M.

Arr. by R. M. McIntosh.

1 A - maz - ing grace!(how sweet the sound!)That sav'd a wretch like me!

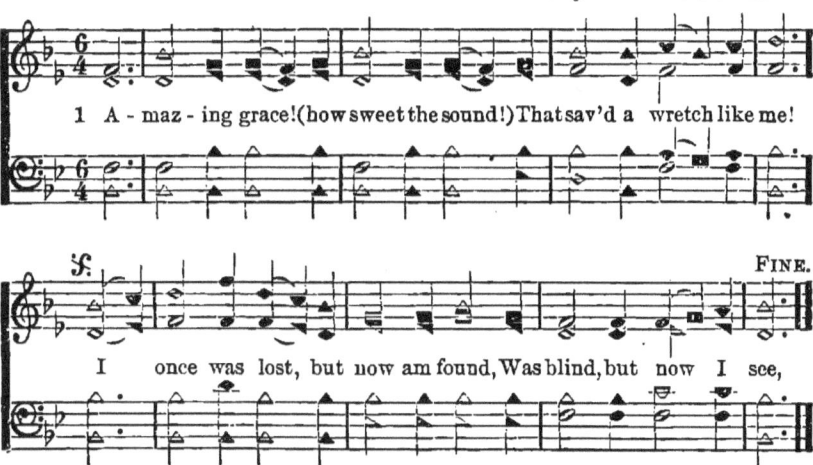

I once was lost, but now am found, Was blind, but now I see,

Close with second strain D. S.

Was blind, but now I see, Was blind, but now I see.

2
'Twas grace that taught my heart to fear,
And grace my fears relieved;
How precious did that grace appear,
The hour I first believed!

3
Through many dangers, toils, and snares,
I have already come;
'Tis grace has brought me safe thus far,
And grace will lead me home.

4
The Lord has promised good to me;
His word my hope secures:
He will my shield and portion be
As long as life endures.

5
Yea, when this flesh and heart shall fail,
And mortal life shall cease,
I shall possess, within the veil,
A life of joy and peace.

No. 22. WORKING WITH THEE.

FRANK M. DAVIS.

1. Work-ing, O Christ, with thee, Work-ing with thee,
   Un-wor-thy, sin-ful, weak, Though we may be,
   Our all to thee we give, For thee a-lone would live,
   And by thy grace a-chieve, Work-ing with thee.

2. A-long the cit-y's waste, Work-ing with thee,
   Our ea-ger foot-steps haste Like thee to be,
   The poor we gath-er in, The out-casts raise from sin,
   And la-bor souls to win, Work-ing with thee.

3. Sav-iour, we wea-ry not, Work-ing with thee,
   As hard as thine own lot, Can nev-er be,
   Our joy and com-fort this, Thy grace suf-fi-cient is,
   This chang-es toil to bliss, Work-ing with thee.

4. So let us la-bor on, Work-ing with thee,
   Till earth to thee is won, From sin set free;
   Till men, from shore to shore, Re-ceive thee and a-dore,
   And join us ev-er-more, Work-ing with thee.

Copyright, 1889, by per. R. M. McIntosh.

No. 24. FOLLOW ME.

F. M. D.   Solo and Chorus.   Frank M. Davis.

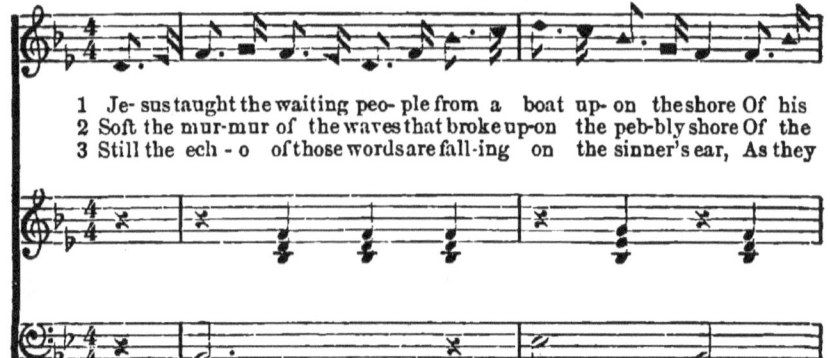

1 Je-sus taught the waiting peo-ple from a boat up-on the shore Of his
2 Soft the mur-mur of the waves that broke up-on the peb-bly shore Of the
3 Still the ech-o of those words are fall-ing on the sinner's ear, As they

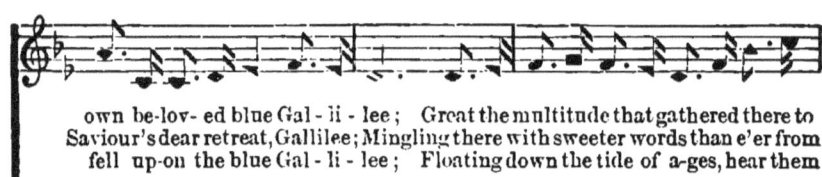

own be-lov-ed blue Gal-li-lee; Great the multitude that gathered there to
Saviour's dear retreat, Gallilee; Mingling there with sweeter words than e'er from
fell up-on the blue Gal-li-lee; Floating down the tide of a-ges, hear them

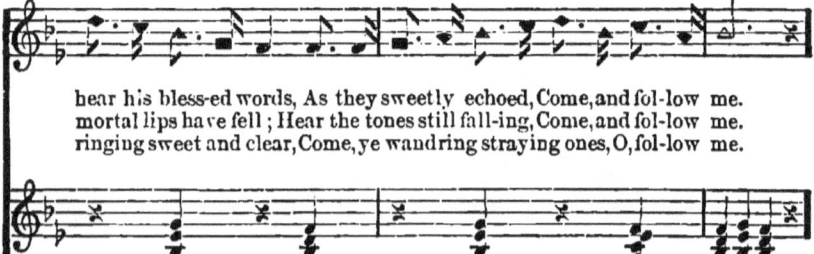

hear his bless-ed words, As they sweetly echoed, Come, and fol-low me.
mortal lips have fell; Hear the tones still fall-ing, Come, and fol-low me.
ringing sweet and clear, Come, ye wand'ring straying ones, O, fol-low me.

Copyright, 1889, by R. M. McIntosh.

No. 26   We Are Marching To The Kingdom.

Mrs. Matilda C. Edwards.   R. M. McIntosh.

1 We are marching to the king-dom, A lit-tle pil-grim band;
2 Through a land of clouds and dark-ness, To bright-est joys a-bove;
3 We have just be-gun the bat-tle, We are fighting for the crown;

And our Cap-tain walks be-fore us, To guide us through the land.
And we have a ban-ner o'er us—The name of it is love.
And we mean to gain the vic-tory Ere we lay our armor down.

CHORUS.

We are marching, we are marching, We are marching to the kingdom,

We are march-ing to the king-dom, A lit-tle pil-grim band.

By per. R. M. McIntosh.

No. 28 GOING HOME.

J. CALVIN BUSHEY.

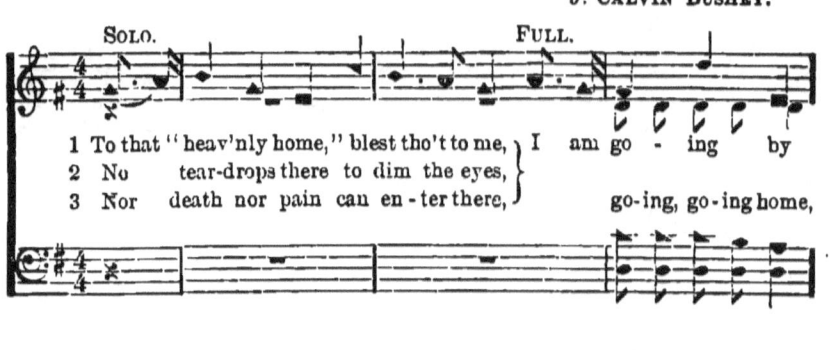

1 To that "heav'nly home," blest tho't to me,
2 No tear-drops there to dim the eyes,
3 Nor death nor pain can en-ter there,

I am go-ing by and by, go-ing, go-ing home,

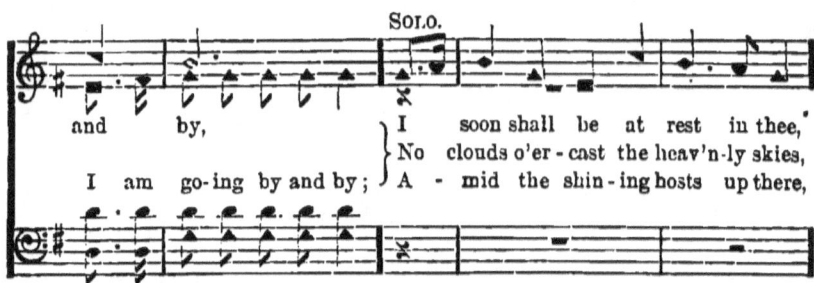

and by, I am go-ing by and by;
{ I soon shall be at rest in thee,
No clouds o'er-cast the heav'n-ly skies,
A-mid the shin-ing hosts up there,

I am go-ing by and by.
go-ing, go-ing home, I am go-ing by and by.

Solo.
Slow, and with strong accent.

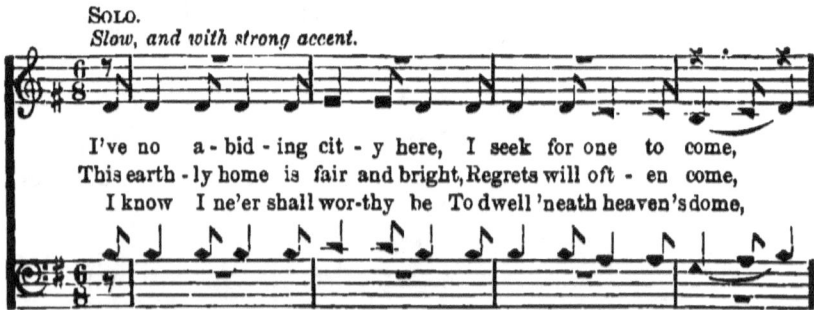

I've no a-bid-ing cit-y here, I seek for one to come,
This earth-ly home is fair and bright, Regrets will oft-en come,
I know I ne'er shall wor-thy be To dwell 'neath heaven's dome,

Copyright, 1885, by R. M. McIntosh.

GOING HOME. Concluded.

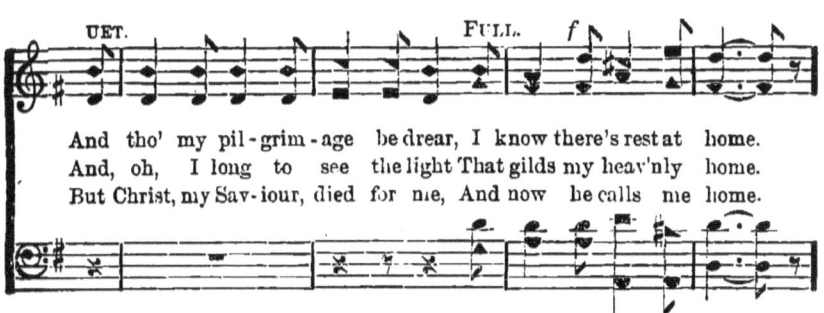

And tho' my pil-grim-age be drear, I know there's rest at home.
And, oh, I long to see the light That gilds my heav'nly home.
But Christ, my Sav-iour, died for me, And now he calls me home.

I am go - ing home by and by, I am
go-ing, go-ing home, go-ing, go-ing home,

go - ing home by and by, by and by; In
go - ing, go - ing home,

heav'n a - bove Where all is love, I'm go - ing by and by.

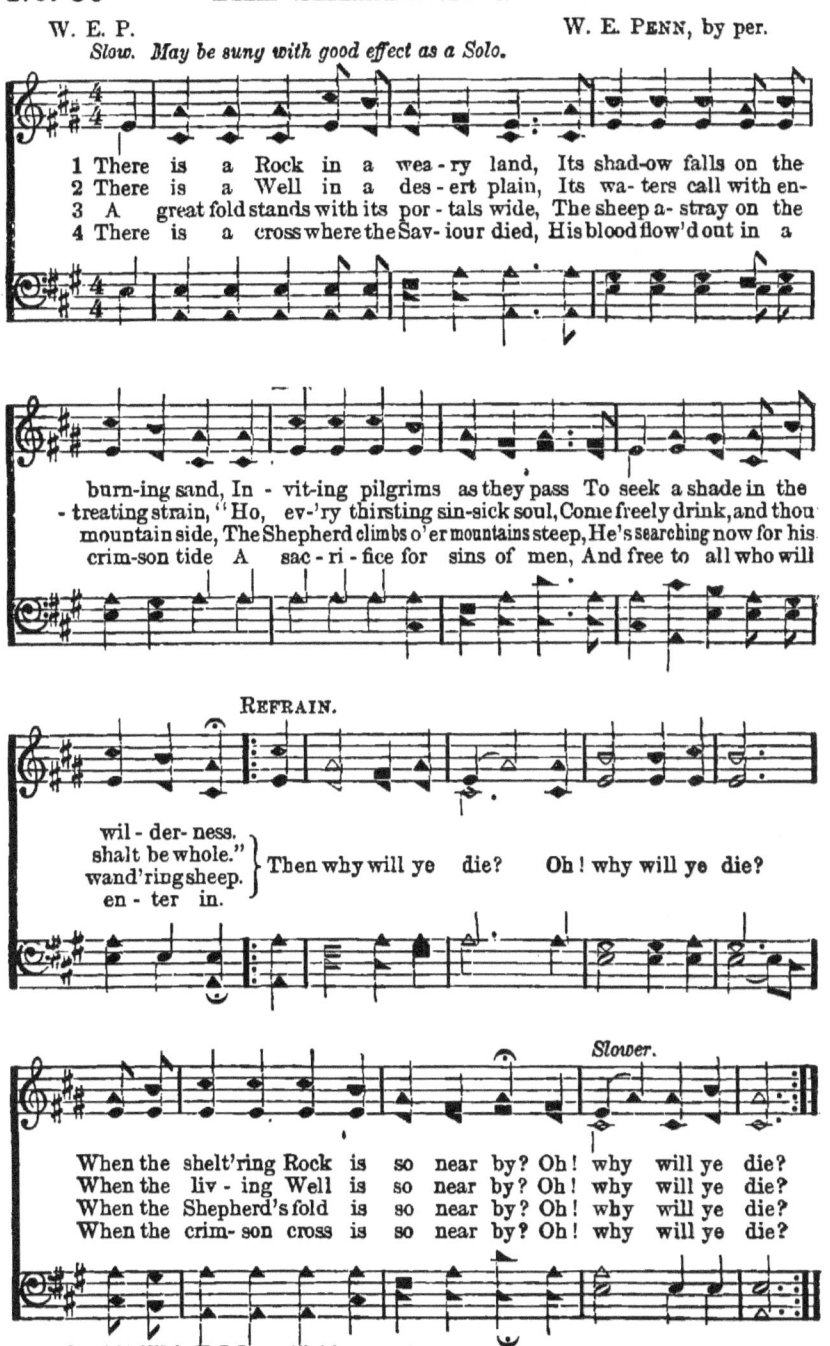

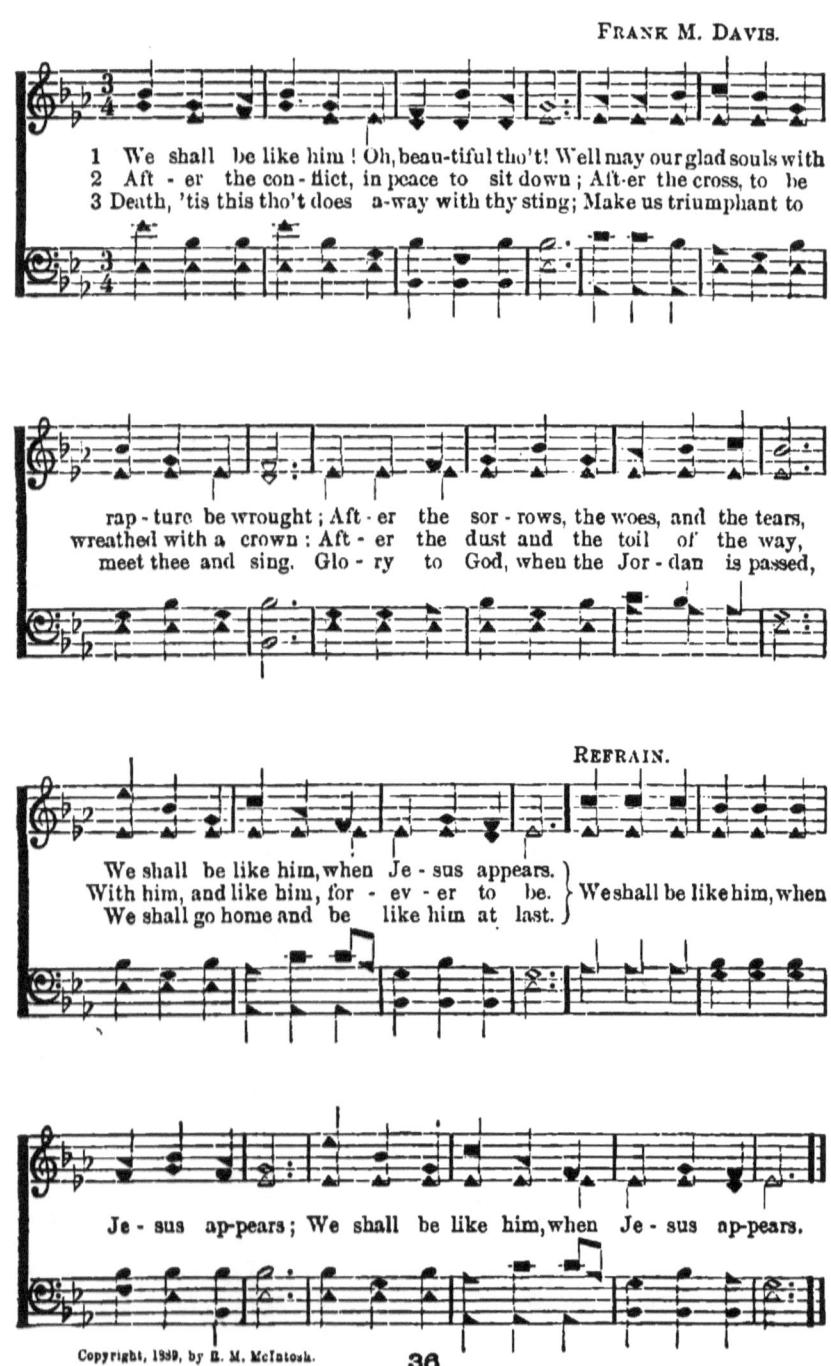

No. 32   They say there's a Land o'er the Ocean.

W. L. T.   W. L. THOMPSON.

1 They say there's a land o'er the o - cean, Where won-ders and beau-ties are seen, They say it's a glo - ri - ous E - den, Where none but the bless - ed con-vene.
2 They say we shall dwell there for - ev - er, If we list to our Saviour's command, They say we shall ev - er be hap - py, When safe in that beau-ti - ful land.
3 They say we shall know all our loved ones, When we meet on that bright, golden shore, They say we shall clasp hands so glad - ly, And to - geth - er re - joice ev - er- more.

By permission of W. L. Thompson & Co., Owners of the Copyright, East Liverpool, Ohio.

They say there's a Land o'er the Ocean. Continued.

They say there's a Land o'er the Ocean. Concluded.

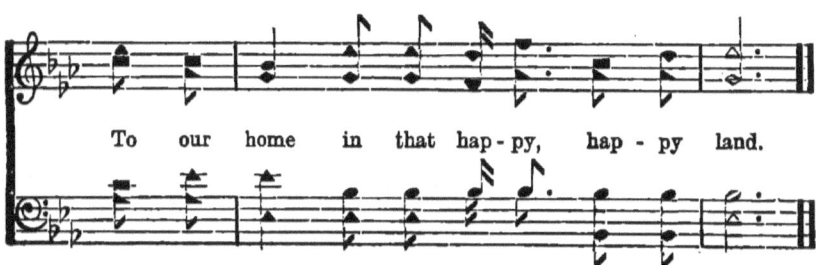

No. 33 I WILL SING WITH JOY.

Rev. J. H. MARTIN, D.D. R. M. McINTOSH.

1. I will lift my voice in a song of praise, To my God and King I'll an an-them raise; By the morn-ing light, in the eve-ning dim, I will sing with joy, I will wor-ship him.

2. I will bless the Lord and ex-tol his name, I will laud his deeds and re-sound his fame; I will sing his pow'r on his throne a-bove, I will glad-ly tell of his grace and love.

3. In the house of God on the day of rest, With a grate-ful heart, with a joy-ful breast, I will sit and sing with the hap-py throng, I will swell the notes of the chor-al song.

REFRAIN.

With the sun by day, and the stars by night, In a glad-some cho-rus at dawn-ing light, I will join with saints and with

Copyright, 1885, by R. M. McIntosh.

I WILL SING WITH JOY. Concluded.

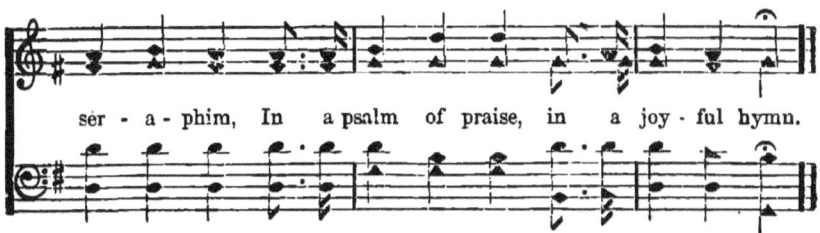

ser-a-phim, In a psalm of praise, in a joy-ful hymn.

No. 34. JESUS, I MY CROSS HAVE TAKEN.

GRANT.   Dr. A. B. EVERETT, by per.

1 { Je - sus, I my cross have tak - en, All to
    Na - ked, poor de - spised, for - sak - en, Thou, from

D.C.—Yet how rich is my con - di - tion, God and

FINE.

leave and fol - low thee: }
hence, my all shalt be. } Per - ish, ev - 'ry fond am-

heav'n are still my own!

D.C.

- bi - tion, All I've sought, or hoped, or known:

2 Let the world despise and leave me:
    They have left my Saviour too:
    Human hearts and looks deceive me—
    Thou art not, like them untrue.
    And while thou shalt smile upon me,
    God of wisdom, love, and might,
    Foes may hate, and friends disown me,
    Show thy face, and all is bright.

3 Go, then, earthly fame and treasure:
    Come, disaster, scorn, and pain:
    In thy service pain is pleasure—
    With thy favor loss is gain.
    I have called thee Abba, Father,—
    I have set my heart on thee,   [er
    Storms may howl, and clouds may gath-
    All must work for good to me.

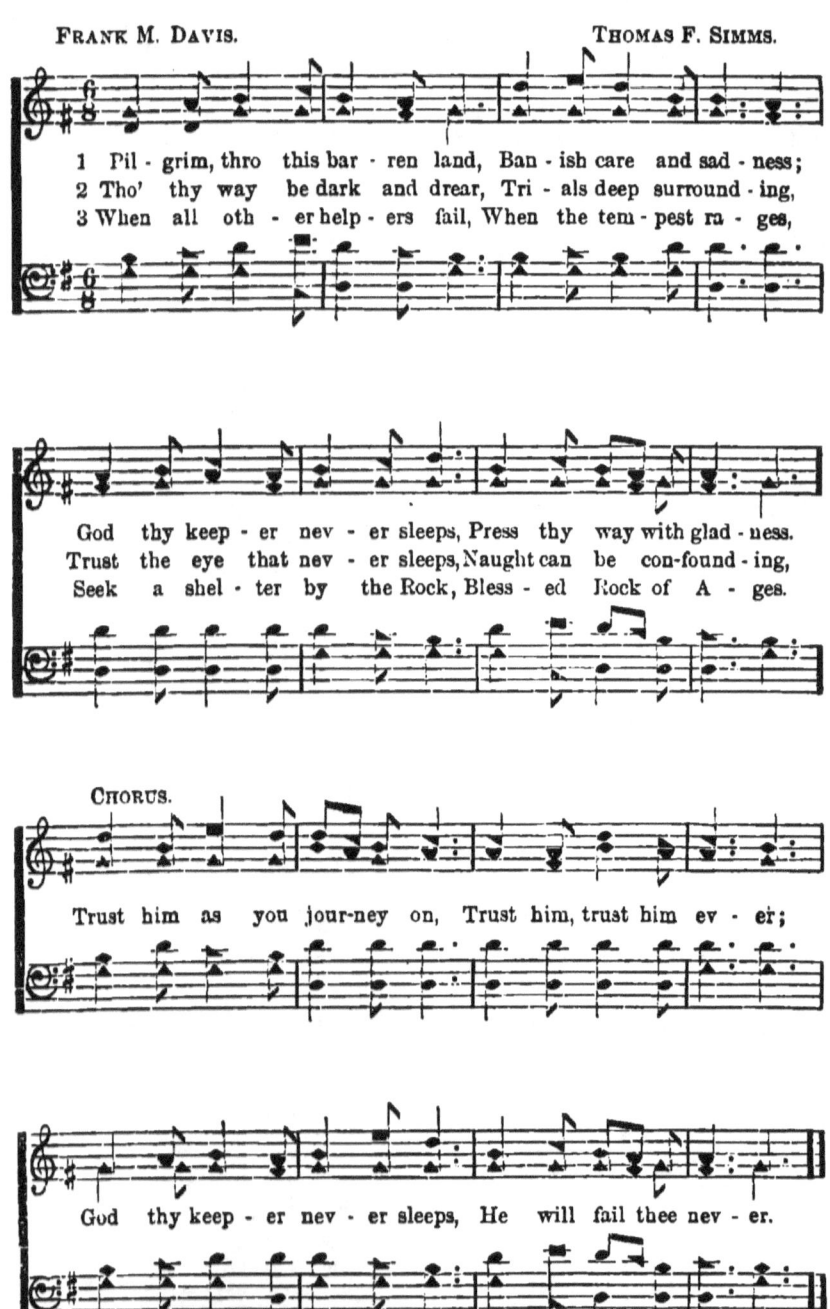

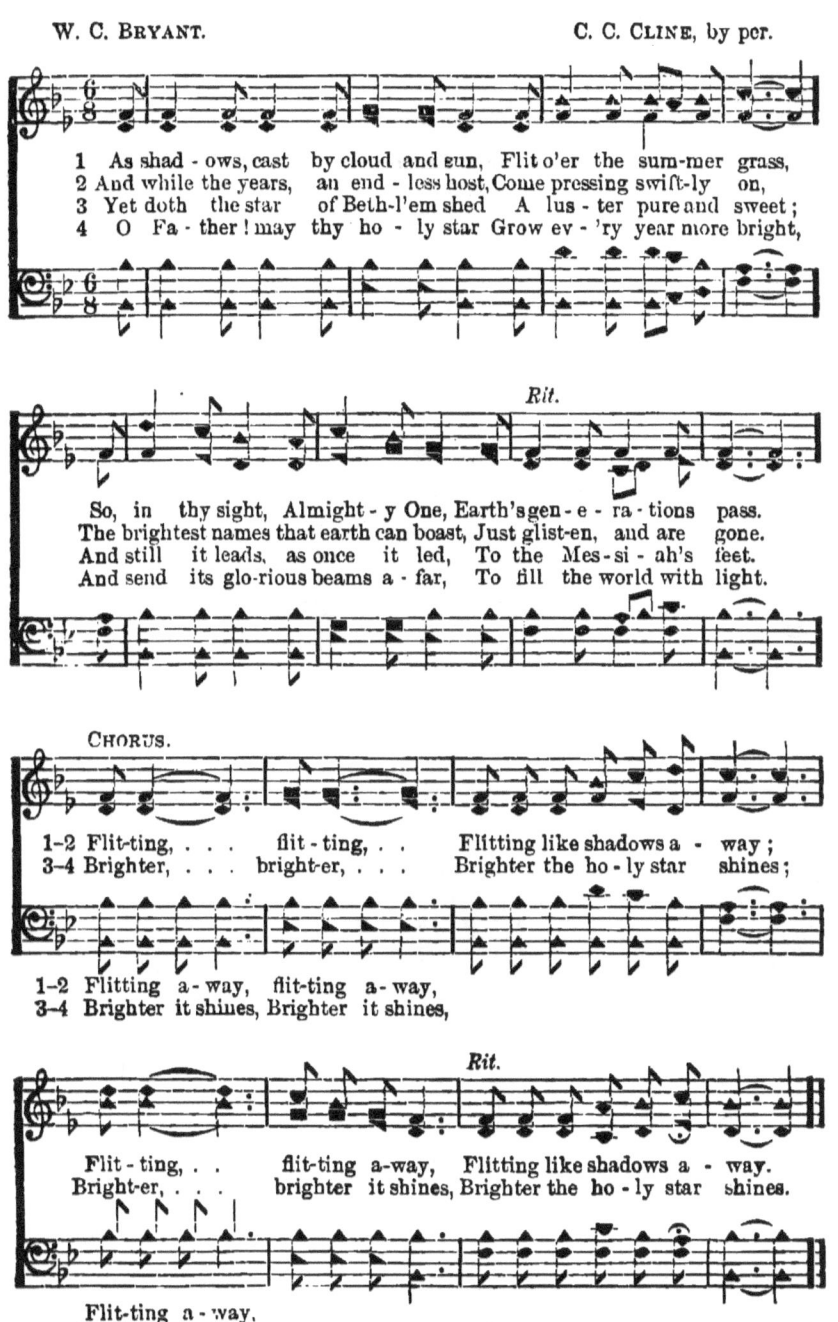

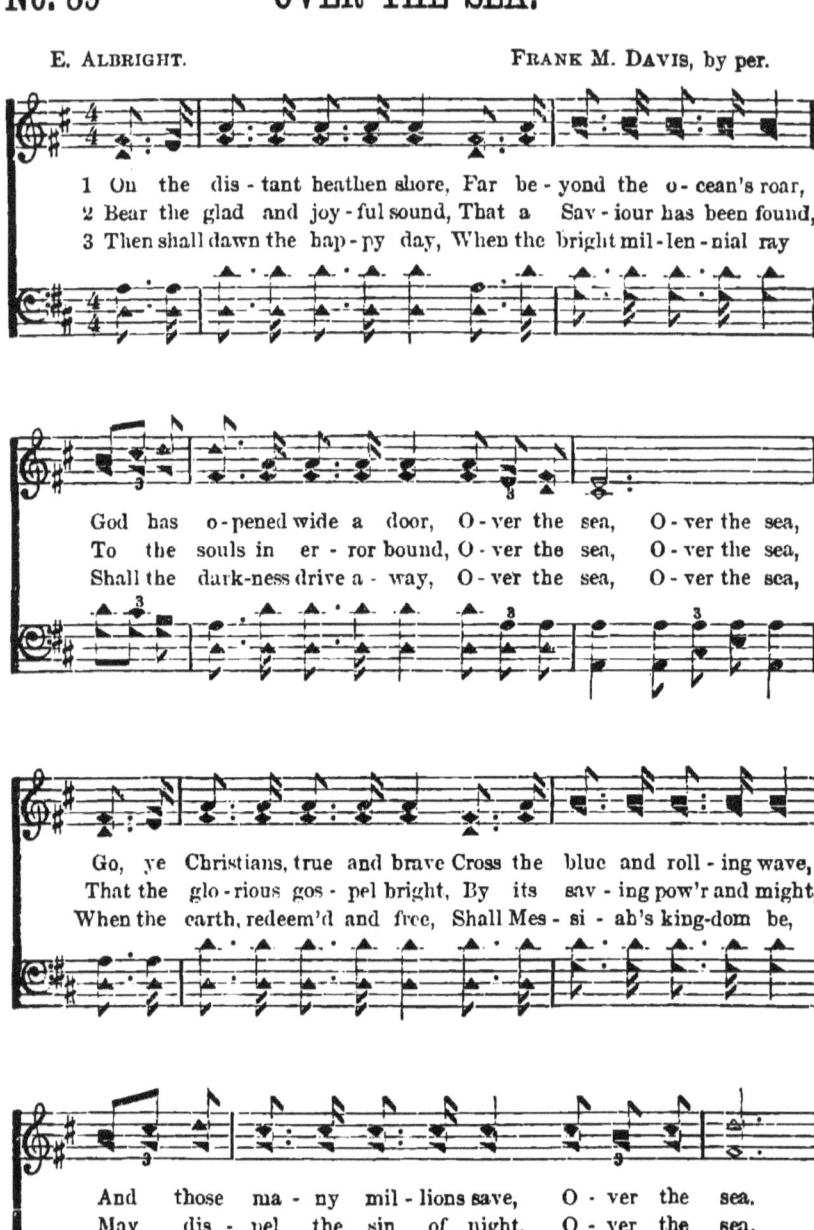

OVER THE SEA. Concluded.

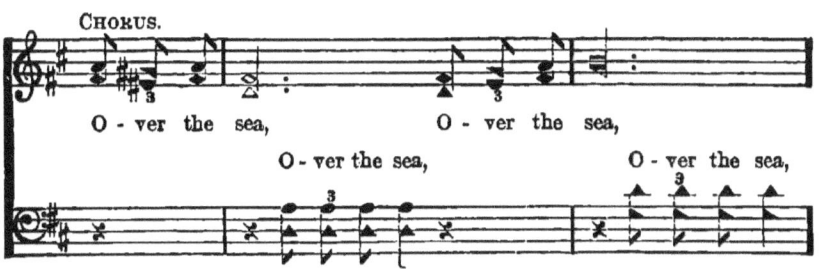

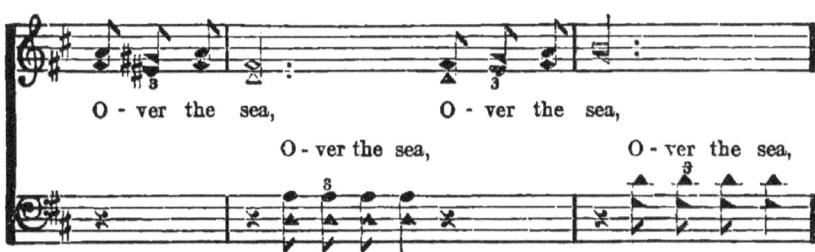

No. 41 THE SWEET STORY.

Rev. J. B. Atchinson. Pearl J. Sprague, by per.

1 Re-peat the sweet sto-ry of Je-sus to me, Oh, tell me the sto-ry once more; Tho' oft-en I've heard it, each time it is told, 'Tis sweeter than ev-er be-fore.
2 Oh, tell me once more of his won-der-ful love, His goodness and mer-cy to me; When hopeless-ly lost in the darkness of sin, He found me and bade me go free.
3 Oh, tell me a-gain of the land of the blest, Where sorrow and sin nev-er come; Where I with the Sav-iour shall ev-er-more dwell, Oh, tell me of heav-en my home.

CHORUS.
'Tis sweet - - - er, yes, sweet - - er each time . . . . . than be-fore, ... Oh, tell me the sto-ry of Je-sus once more, 'Tis sweet-er, yes, sweet-er each time than before; Then tell . . . me the sto - - ry of Je - - sus once more.

1 How he died on the tree for sinners like me, Oh, tell me the story of Jesus once more.
2 How his wonderful love bro't him from above.
3 Where I with the blest shall evermore rest.

49

No. 42. Shall We Know Each Other There.

Mrs. ANNIE E. THOMSON. FRANK M. DAVIS.

1 When we've cross'd death's solemn river, When this troubled life is o'er,
2 Shall we meet our saint-ed mother, Who for ma-ny years hath slept,
3 Shall we see them robed in splendor, With no shad-ows on their brow,
4 He who soothes us in af-flictions, He whose love doth ne'er de-part,

And we go to dwell for-ev-er, Where the wea-ry weep no more;
Fa-ther, sis-ter dear, and brother, Whom we oft have mourn'd and wept?
Meet their lov-ing smiles so ten-der; Which our hearts are crav-ing now,
Breath his heavenly ben-e-dictions, O'er each griev'd and wounded heart;

In those bright and heavenly pla-ces, Where the skies are al-ways fair,
Those un-to our hearts yet dear-er, Who our griefs were wont to share;
List to tones whose mu-sic on-ly Chased a-way each shade of care;
He who's left such bless-ed promise, Gives us bliss be-yond com-pare;

Shall we greet fa-mil-iar fa-ces? Shall we know each oth-er there?
In that fade-less light and clearer, Shall we know each oth-er there?
That have left the world so lone-ly, Shall we know each oth-er there?
He this joy will not take from us, We shall know each oth-er there.

Copyright, 1889, by R. M. McIntosh.

Shall We Know Each Other There. Concluded.

HE'S WATCHING O'ER ME. Concluded.

watch-ing o'er me, And call-ing me, call-ing me home.

No. 44. ANTIOCH. C. M.

1. Joy to the world, the Lord is come! Let earth re-ceive her King;
2. Joy to the earth, the Sav-iour reigns! Let men their songs em-ploy;

Let ev-'ry heart pre-pare him room, And heav'n and na-ture sing.
While fields and floods, rocks, hill, and plains, Re-peat the sounding joy.

And heav'n and na-
Re-peat the sound-

And heav'n and na-ture sing, And heav'n, and heav'n and na-ture sing.
Re-peat the sounding joy, Re-peat, re-peat the sounding joy.
-ture sing, ...
-ing joy, ...

-ture sing, And heav'n and nature sing, And heav'n and na-ture sing.
-ing joy, Re-peat the sounding joy, Re-peat the sound-ing joy.

3 No more let sins and sorrows grow,
Nor thorns infest the ground:
He comes to make his blessings flow,
Far as the curse is found.

4 He rules the world with truth and grace;
And makes the nations prove
The glories of his righteousness,
And wonders of his love.

THE BARREN FIG-TREE. Concluded.

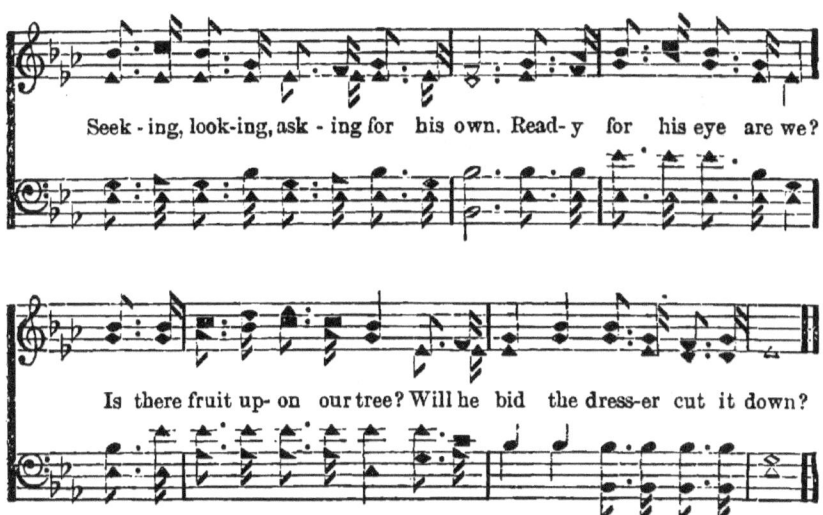

Seek-ing, look-ing, ask-ing for his own. Read-y for his eye are we?

Is there fruit up-on our tree? Will he bid the dress-er cut it down?

No. 50.   ROCK OF AGES.   7s.   6 lines.

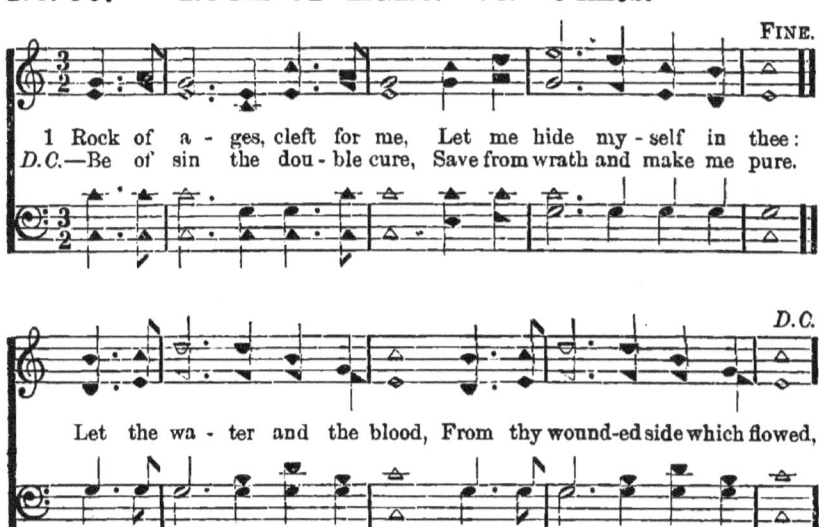

1 Rock of a - ges, cleft for me, Let me hide my - self in thee:
D.C.—Be of' sin the dou - ble cure, Save from wrath and make me pure.

Let the wa - ter and the blood, From thy wound-ed side which flowed,

2 Could my tears forever flow,
Could my zeal no languor know,
These for sin could not atone;
Thou must save, and thou alone:
In my hand no price I bring,
Simply to thy cross I cling.

3 While I draw this fleeting breath,
When my eyes shall close in death,
When I rise to worlds unknown,
And behold thee on thy throne,
Rock of ages, cleft for me,
Let me hide myself in thee.

No. 51   WE'LL GATHER THEM IN.

Rev. E. A. Hoffman.   R. M. McIntosh.

1 We'll gath-er the chil-dren of want and sin Out of dark-ness and out of gloom; We'll bring them in joy to the Master's home; In his house there is ample room.
2 We'll gath-er them in to the roy-al feast, Where the bounties of grace are spread, Where perishing souls with the bread of life In the ten-der-est love are fed.
3 We'll gath-er the halt, and the sick and blind, From the wear-i-some paths of sin, To Jesus, their Saviour and loving Friend, We will gather these lost ones in.
4 We'll gath-er the sad and the wear-y ones To the feet of the bless-ed Lord; He'll pardon their sin and renew their hearts; 'Tis the hope of his precious Word.

REFRAIN.

We will gath-er them in to the feast of the King, From the highways and by-ways of sin, From the hedg-es and the lanes, From the mountains and the plains, We will gather wear-y trav'lers in.

Copyright, 1889, by R. M. McIntosh.

IT IS BETTER FURTHER ON. Concluded.

2 Hope is singing, still is singing,
   Softly in an under tone;
   Singing as if God had taught it,
   "It is better further on."

3 Night and day it sings the same song,
   Sings it when I sit alone;
   Sings it so the heart may hear it,
   "It is better further on."

4 On the grave it sits and sings it,
   Sings it when the heart would groan;
   Sings it when the shadows darken,
   "It is better further on."

5 Further on! Oh! how much further?
   Count the mile-stones one by one;
   No! no counting, only trusting,
   "It is better further on."

Walk in the Marvelous Light. Concluded.

Walk.... in the light.... Walk.... in the
Walk in the light, the mar-vel-ous light, Walk in the light, the

light, Walk in the mar-vel-ous light, the light of God.
mar-velous light,

No. 55. ARLINGTON. C. M.

1 Once more we come be - fore our God; Once more his bless-ings ask:
2 Fa - ther, thy quick'ning Spir - it send From heav'n in Je - sus' Name,
3 May we re-ceive the word we hear, Each in an hon - est heart;
4 To seek thee all our hearts dis-pose, To each thy blessings suit,

O may not du - ty seem a load, Nor worship prove a task!
To make our wait - ing minds at-tend, And put our souls in frame.
And keep the pre - cious treas-ure there, And nev - er with it part.
And let the seed thy ser-vant sows Pro - duce a - bun-dant fruit.

GO GATHER THE GOLDEN GRAIN. Concluded.

ripe with the har-vest, Go gath-er the gold-en grain.

No. 59. **TAKE ME AS I AM.**

R. M. McIntosh.

1 Je-sus, my Lord, to thee I cry, Un-less thou help me I must die;
2 Help-less I am, and full of guilt, But yet for me thy blood was spilt,
3 If thou hast work for me to do, In-spire my will, my heart re-new,
4 And when at last the work is done, The bat-tle o'er, the vict'ry won,

Oh, bring thy free sal-va-tion nigh, And take me as I am.
And thou can'st make me what thou wilt, But take me as I am.
And work both in and by me, too, But take me as I am.
Still, still my cry shall be a-lone, Oh, take me as I am.

D.S.—Oh, bring thy free sal-va-tion nigh, And take me as I am.

REFRAIN.

Take me as I am, ... Take me as I am, ...
Take me, take me as I am, Take me, take me as I am,

Copyright, 1885, by R. M. McIntosh.

When the Mists have Cleared away. Concluded.

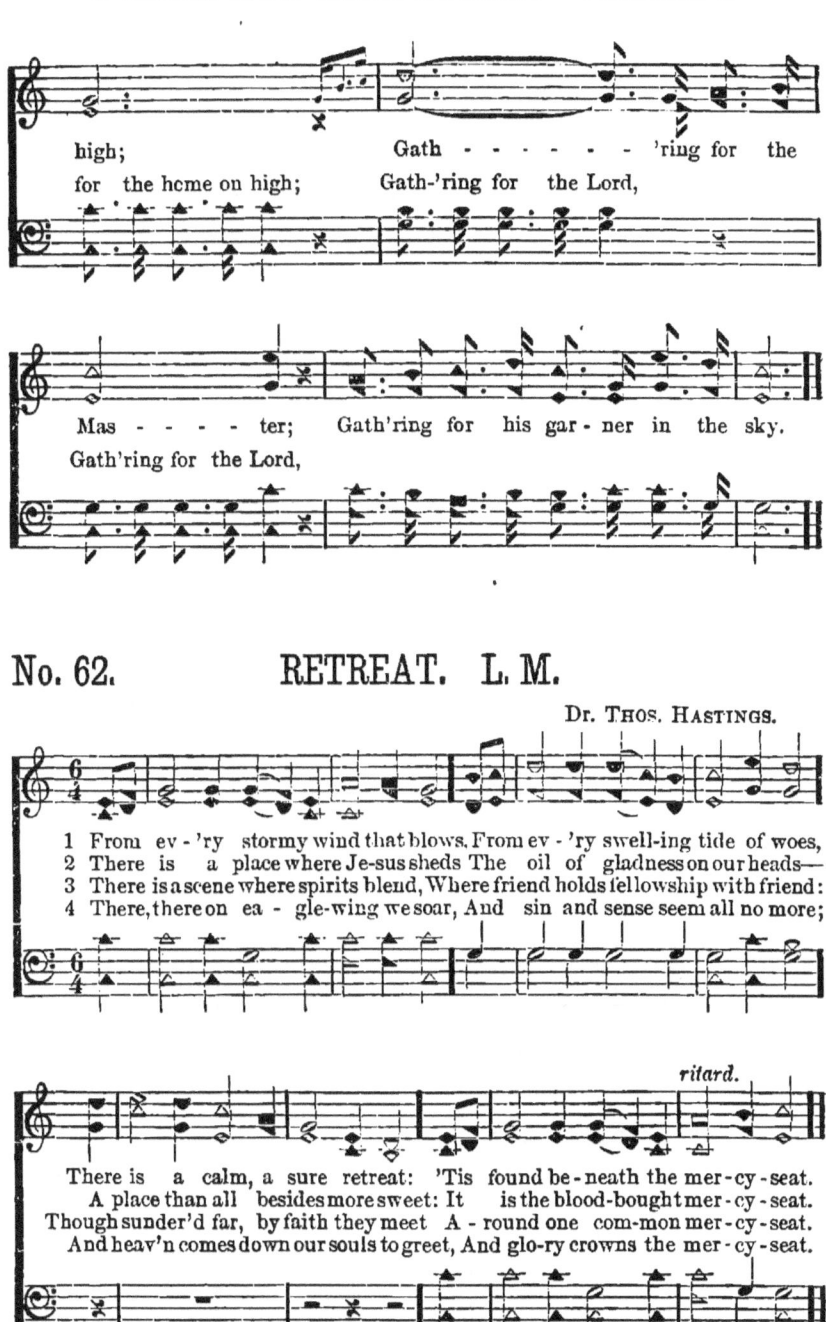

No. 63. THE WELCOME REFRAIN.

Rev. J. H. Martin, D. D.   R. M. McIntosh.

1. Hear the jubilant song that the seraphim sang, When at
midnight the air with sweet melody rang, As the
heralds of heaven glad tidings they bring, For they publish the
birth of a Saviour and King.

2. 'Twas a hymn of salvation that echoed around, And the
shepherds first heard the sweet, wonderful sound; But it
rolls thro' the earth and the ages of time, As a chorus of
gladness, an anthem sublime.

REFRAIN.

Hear the song, hear the song, hear the song, Hear the song by angels
Hear the song, hear the song, Hear the song by angels

Copyright, 1885, by R. M. McIntosh.

THE WELCOME REFRAIN. Concluded.

No. 64 SOME DAY.

EBEN E. REXFORD.
FRANK M. DAVIS, by per.
DUET.

1 I hear a song, a song so sweet, I try all
2 Some day my jour-ney will be done, Earth will be
3 Some day I say, con-tent to wait The op'-ning
4 When comes the time for me to go, The home-ward

vain-ly to re-peat; Its mel-o-dy and feel-ing
lost and heav-en won; And when the long rough way is
of the jas-per gate; Come soon or late, that day will
path I may not know, But in God's hand my own I'll

say, I'll sing it if God wills some day.
trod, I shall be-hold the face of God.
be The dawn of end-less rest to me.
lay, And he will lead me home some day.

CHORUS.

Some day, some hap-py day to be, My voice will learn its mel-o-
Some happy day. a day to be, My voice will learn its

SOME DAY. Concluded.

- dy, And I shall sing the songs so sweet, Of rest and heav'n, at Jesus' feet.
mel-o-dy.

No. 65. ENOUGH FOR ME.

E. A. H.   Rev. E. A. Hoffman, by per.

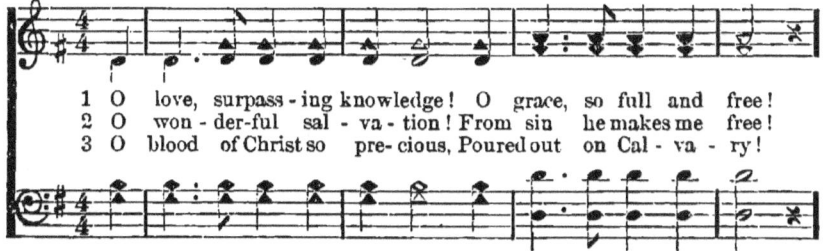

1. O love, surpass-ing knowledge! O grace, so full and free!
2. O won-der-ful sal-va-tion! From sin he makes me free!
3. O blood of Christ so pre-cious, Poured out on Cal-va-ry!

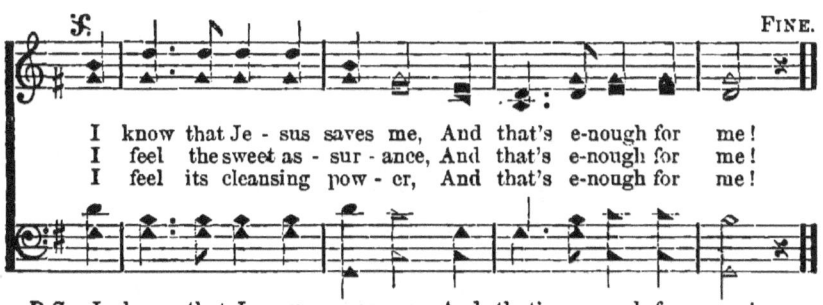

I know that Je-sus saves me, And that's e-nough for me!
I feel the sweet as-sur-ance, And that's e-nough for me!
I feel its cleansing pow-er, And that's e-nough for me!

D.S.—I know that Je-sus saves me, And that's e-nough for me!

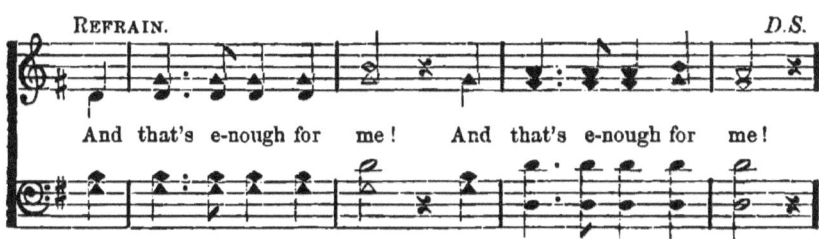

And that's e-nough for me! And that's e-nough for me!

SWEET REST. Concluded.

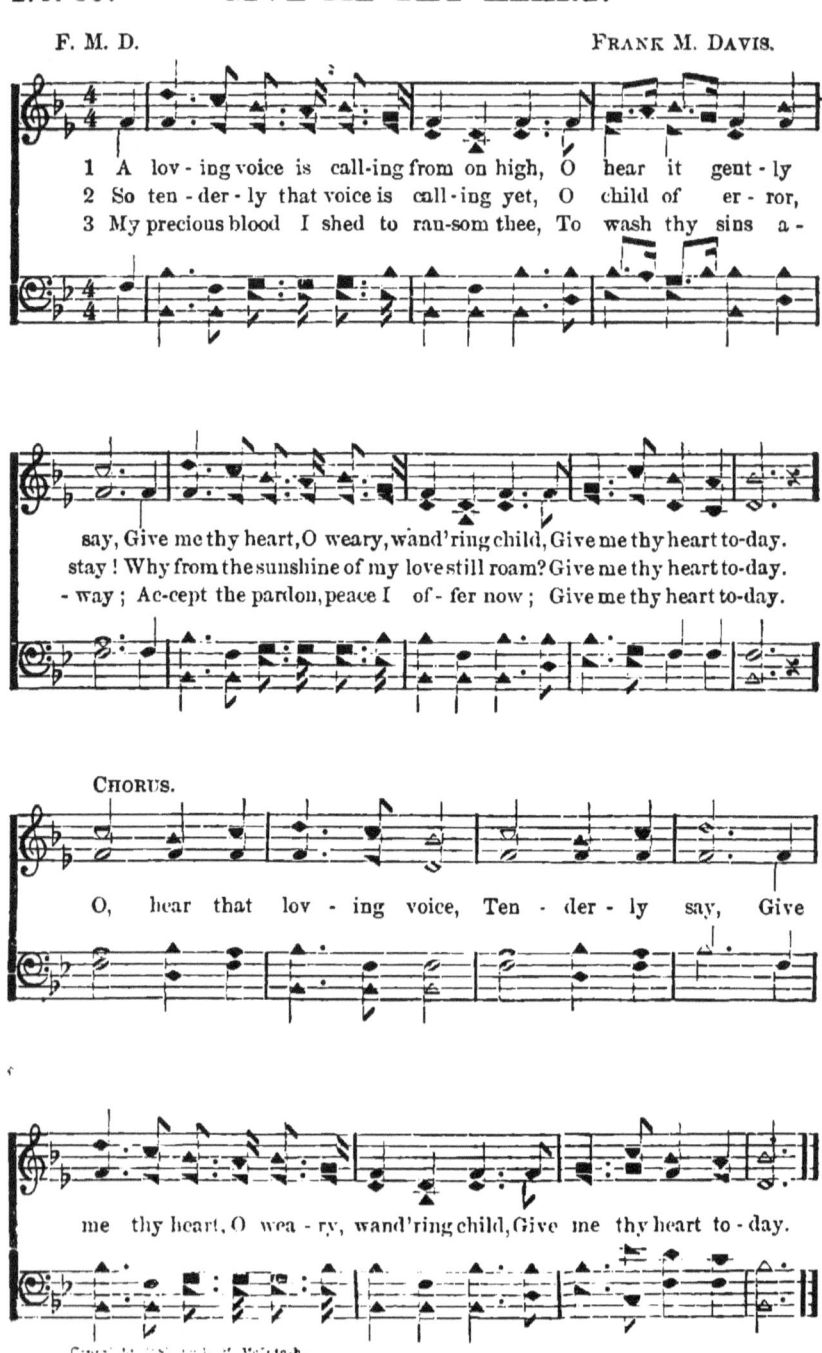

No. 70 DAY-BREAK.

ANNIE HERBERT.
May be used as a SOLO.
F. A. BLACKMER.

1 When the clouds have left the hill-tops, And the beau-ty of the day Gleams a-long through gold-en por-tals, Melt-ing all the mists a-way, Then no more will shad-ows dark-en, Till the way we can-not see—

2 When the dark-ness rolls from o-cean, And the light beams bright-ly o'er Ev-'ry wave and foam-ing bil-low, Dash-ing 'gainst this mor-tal shore, Then the heart will sing with rapt-ure, And the voice break forth in praise

3 When the pain and wast-ing fe-ver, And the thou-sand ills of life, All are healed by one Phy-si-cian, And for-ev-er hushed the strife, Then sweet peace and ho-ly com-fort Will pos-sess the in-most soul,

4 When the graves of earth are o-pened, And the fair, lov'd forms a-rise, Spring-ing up from dust-y cham-bers, Soar-ing up-ward to the skies, Then sweet waves of thrill-ing mu-sic Will en-trance the list-'ning ear,

5 When the Cit-y, grand, e-ter-nal, Shall de-scend 'mid clouds of light, And the King bids saints to en-ter Man-sions filled with ho-ly light, Then the life-work of all a-ges Will re-ceive a just re-ward,

Copyright, 1884, by F. A. Blackmer.

DAY-BREAK. Concluded.

85

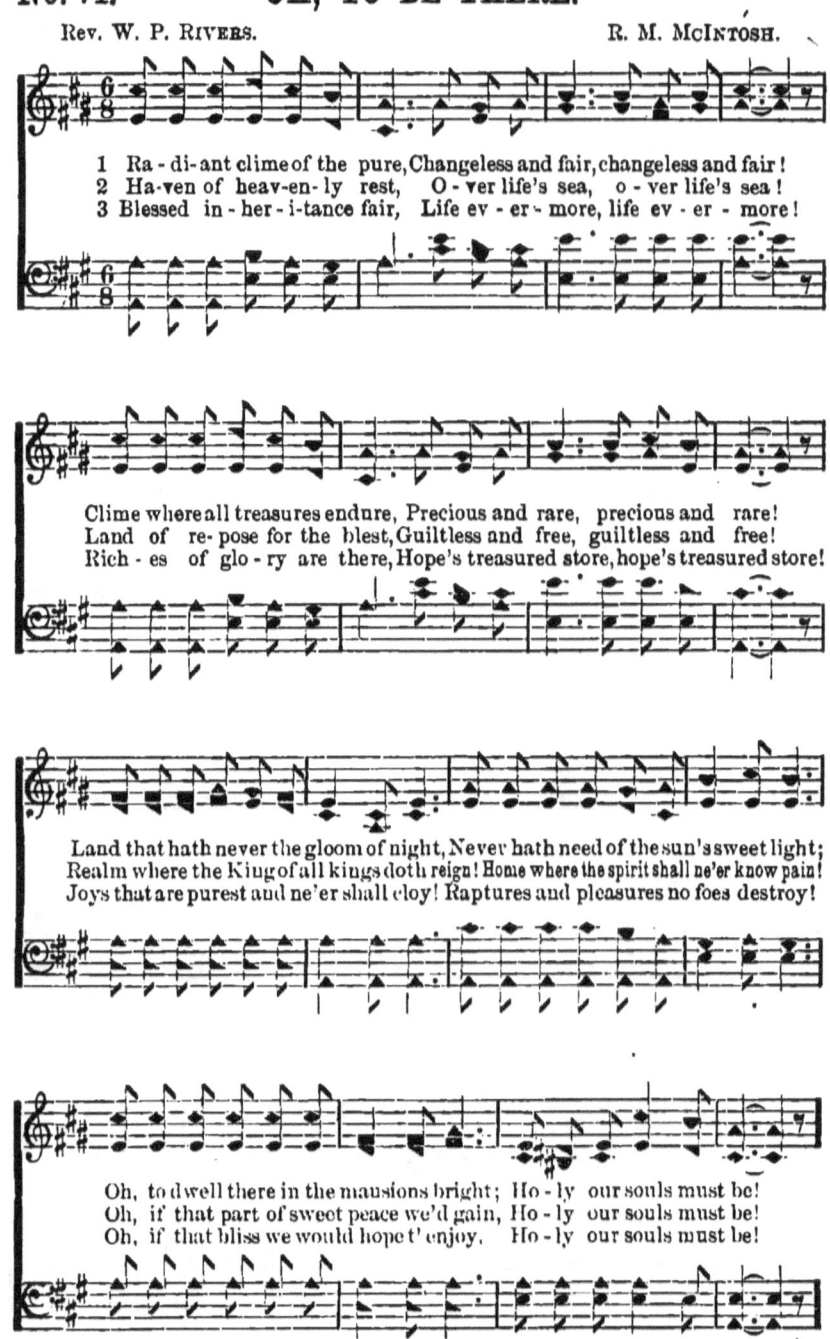

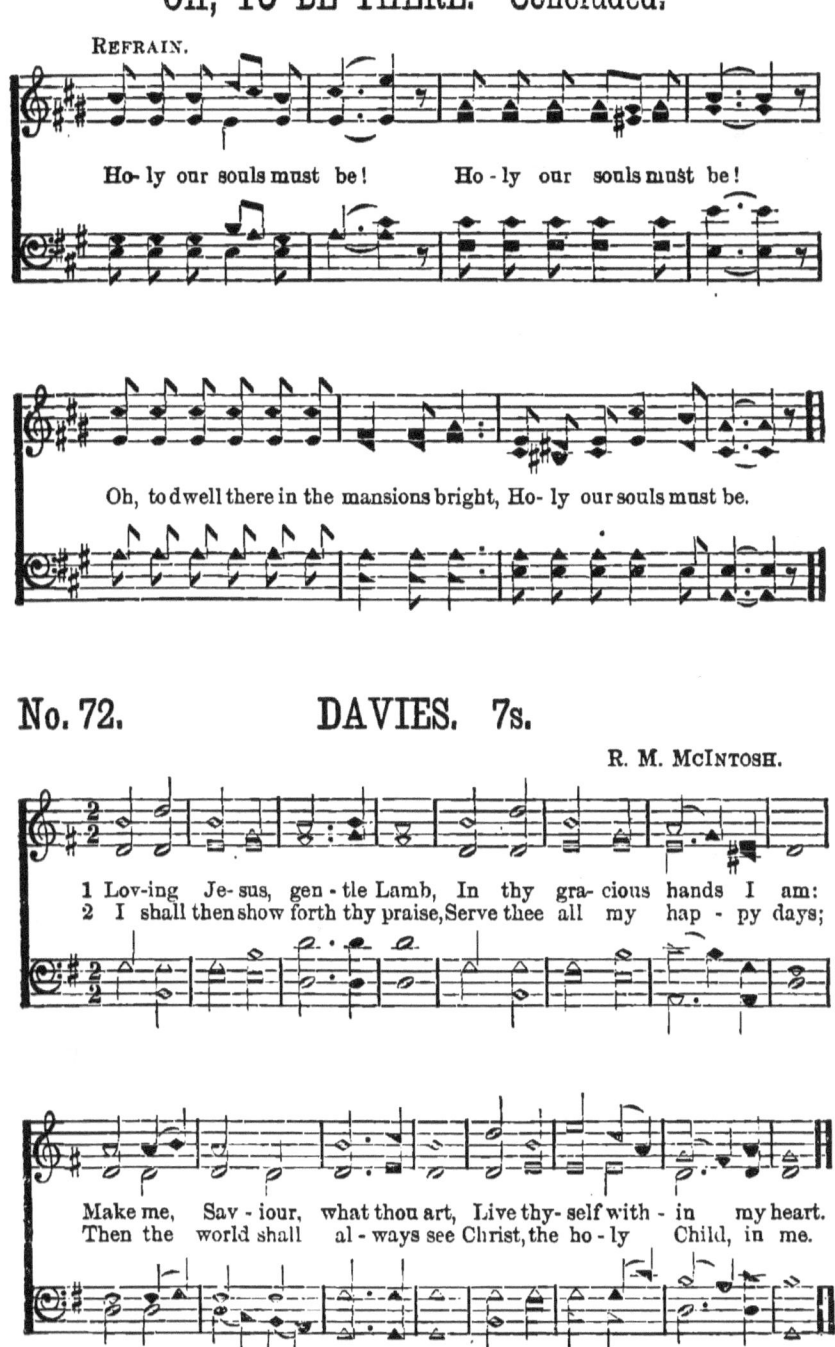

No. 73. PRESS ONWARD!

Mrs. Estelle Oltrogge. Mrs. Estelle Oltrogge.

1 Press on-ward, oh, Christian, and leave not the race, You must val-ient-ly fight ere you see God's face; He's promised to give you his grace, day by day; So ask him for help, and go on your way.

2 The tempt-er may smile as an an-gel of light, While he tempts you a-way from the paths of right; Our Sav-iour was tempt-ed, but bade Sa-tan flee, And brought free sal-va-tion for you and me.

3 Your sor-rows and tri-als may now weigh you down; But you must bear the Cross if you'd wear the Crown; The wear-y and lad-en who come to the Lord, Find rest, this we know from his Ho-ly Word.

REFRAIN.

Sing then, sing then, sing as on you go, Joy-ful, joy-ful journey here be-low; The way may be toilsome while here you a-bide,—But, oh, there is rest on the oth-er side.

Copyright, 1889, by R. M. McIntosh.

No. 75. The Marriage of the King's Son.

Mrs. M. B. C. Slade.   R. M. McIntosh.

1 Once a feast was made and the board was laid, And the king ar-ray'd in his gar-ments fair; For my son, said he, shall the glad feast be; Bear my mes-sage free, bid the guests be there.
2 Forth a-gain he sent and his serv-ants went To the bid-den guests, but they turned a-way; Then the king was wroth, and he hast-ened forth, And the sounds of wrath filled the fes-tal day.
3 Once a-gain he cried, for my feast sup-plied, From the high-way side, gath-er one and all. Lo, they quick-ly haste to the mar-riage feast, To each low-ly guest 'tis a wel-come call.
4 When our King shall call, may we one and all, In his pal-ace hall haste to take our seat; Wedding gar-ments fair love and grace pre-pare, We'll re-joic-ing wear, when the King we meet.

CHORUS.

When for you and me such a call shall be, When the King cries come, shall we joy-ful rise and go? Oh re-joice, re-joice, for I

By per. R. M. McIntosh.

The Marriage of the King's Son. Concluded.

hear his voice, To his feast we'll haste, for he loves us so.

No. 76. UNSEARCHABLE RICHES.

F. J. C.   J. R. SWENEY, by per.

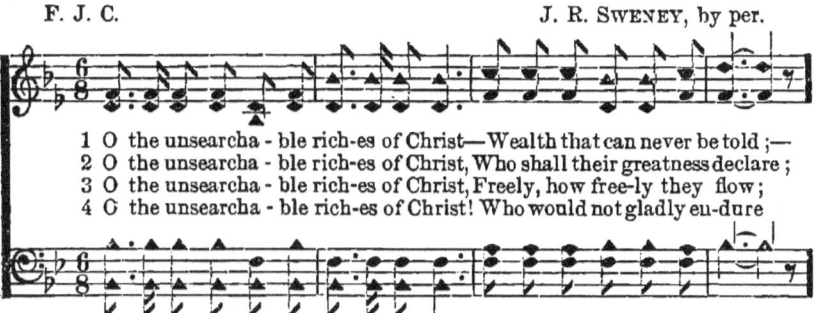

1 O the unsearcha - ble rich-es of Christ—Wealth that can never be told;—
2 O the unsearcha - ble rich-es of Christ, Who shall their greatness declare;
3 O the unsearcha - ble rich-es of Christ, Freely, how free-ly they flow;
4 O the unsearcha - ble rich-es of Christ! Who would not gladly en-dure

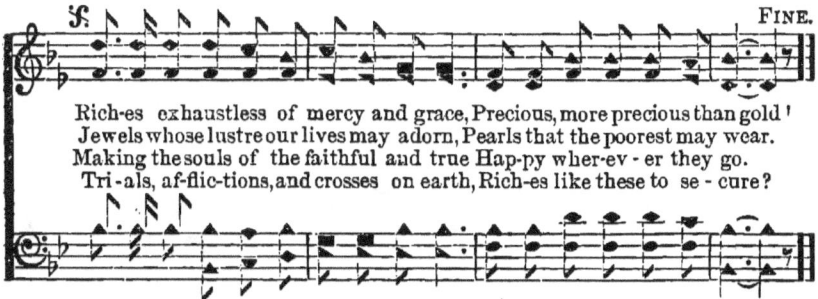

Rich-es exhaustless of mercy and grace, Precious, more precious than gold!
Jewels whose lustre our lives may adorn, Pearls that the poorest may wear.
Making the souls of the faithful and true Hap-py wher-ev - er they go.
Tri-als, af-flic-tions, and crosses on earth, Rich-es like these to se - cure?

D.S.—O the unsearcha - ble riches of Christ! Precious, more precious than gold.

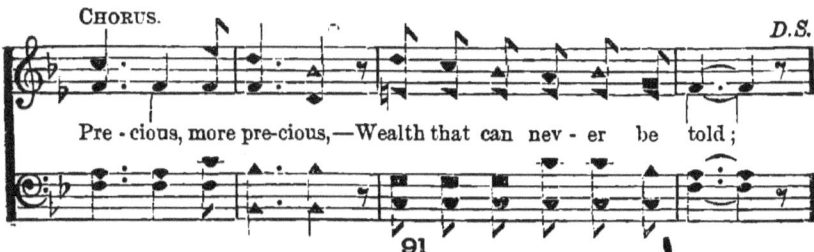

Pre - cious, more pre-cious,—Wealth that can nev - er be told;

No. 80. WONDERFUL WORDS FOR ALL.

F. M. D. FRANK M. DAVIS.

1 Wonder-ful words, God has spo-ken; Won-derful words, thro' his Son!
2 Wonder-ful words, to the wea-ry; Come, heavy la-den ones, come!
3 Wonder-ful words, to the seek-er; Ask in my name, and re-ceive;

He who-so-ev-er be-liev-eth, Life ev-er-last-ing has won!
You shall find rest, saith the spir-it, Rest in my heaven-ly home.
Joy and sal-va-tion a-waits you; If you on me will be-lieve.

CHORUS.

Wonder-ful words, God has spo-ken, Won-der-ful words to all;

Words that will nev-er be bro-ken; Wonder-ful words to all.

Copyright, 1889, by R. M. McIntosh.

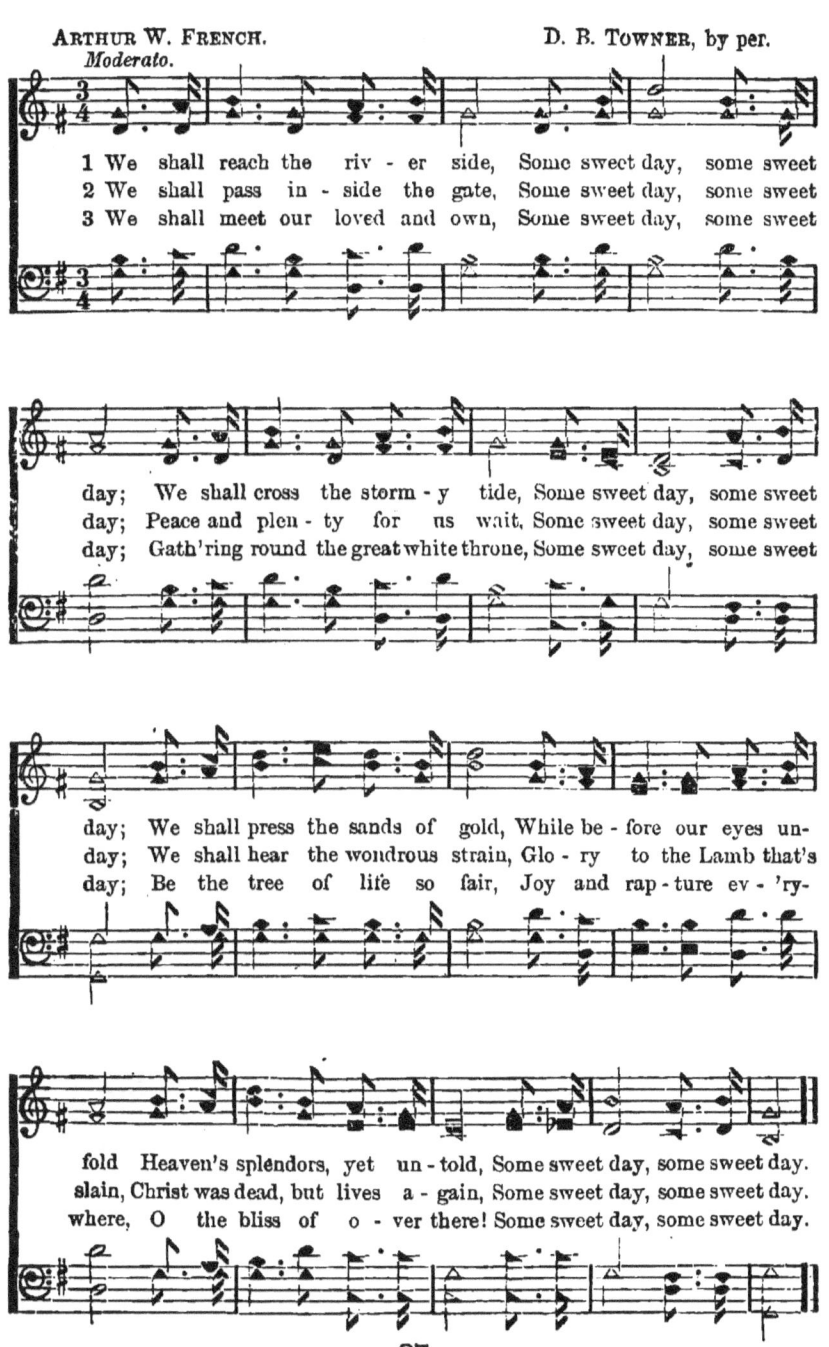

HOSANNA. Continued.

HOSANNA. Concluded.

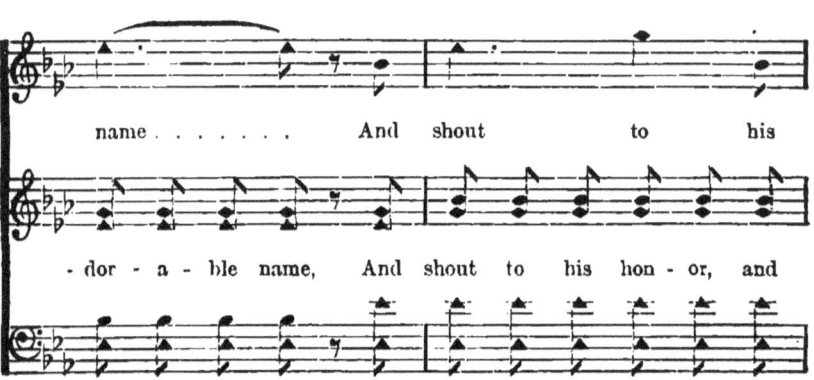

No. 84. WHERE SHALL WE GO?

F. M. D.
FRANK M. DAVIS.

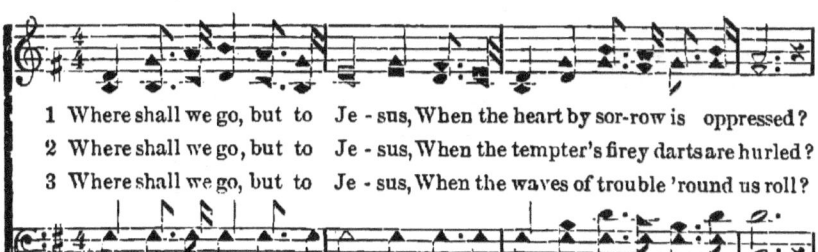

1 Where shall we go, but to Je-sus, When the heart by sor-row is oppressed?
2 Where shall we go, but to Je-sus, When the tempter's firey darts are hurled?
3 Where shall we go, but to Je-sus, When the waves of trouble 'round us roll?

Where shall we flee from the tem-pest, But to him for shel-ter and for rest?
Who can give strength in our weakness, But the Sav-iour of this dy-ing world?
Who, but the Saviour, can lead us To the glorious home-land of the soul?

CHORUS.

Where shall we go? Where shall we go? Where shall we go, but to Je - sus?

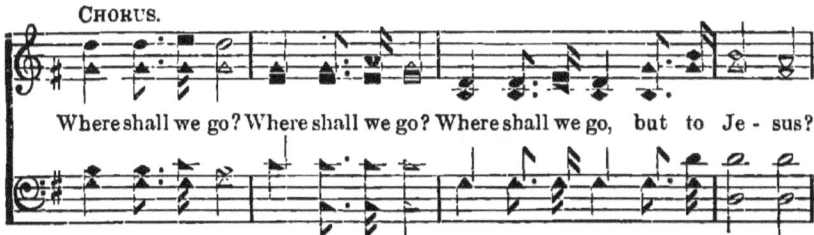

Where shall we go? Where shall we go? Where shall we go, but to Je - sus?

Copyright, 1889, by per. R. M. McIntosh.

JOYOUSLY ON. Concluded.

We are march-ing on, to Ca-naan's hap-py land. (hap-py land.)

No. 86. RICHMOND. S. M. Double.

Dr. A. B. EVERETT, by per.

1 A charge to keep I have, A God to glo-ri-fy;
2 Arm me with jeal-ous care, As in thy sight to live:

A nev-er-dy-ing-soul to save, And fit it for the sky;
And O, thy ser-vant, Lord, pre-pare A strict ac-count to give!

D.S.—O may it all my powers en-gage To do my Mas-ter's will!
As-sured if, I my trust be-tray, I shall for-ev-er die.

To serve the pres-ent age, My call-ing to ful-fil;
Help me to watch and pray, And on thy-self re-ly,

THE LORD IS MY SHEPHERD. Concluded.

No. 89   PRECIOUS WORDS.

Mrs. LOULA K. ROGERS.   R. M. McINTOSH.

1. Precious for-ev-er! oh, wonderful words, Teach me the pathway of du-ty; Lead me beside the still waters of life, Flowing through valleys of beauty.
2. Freely he offers their promise to all, "Come un-to me whosoever," Sinners oppressed with a burden of woe, Drink of the bountiful river.
3. Wouldst thou refuse the sweet solace he gives, In the midnight of thy sorrow? Wouldst thou go on in the darkness of sin, Longing for no bright tomorrow?

REFRAIN.

Precious forever to you and to me, Words that our Saviour has spoken, Bearing salvation far over the sea, Healing the hearts that are broken!

No. 90. THE MESSAGE OF SALVATION.

C. H. G. CHAS. H. GABRIEL.

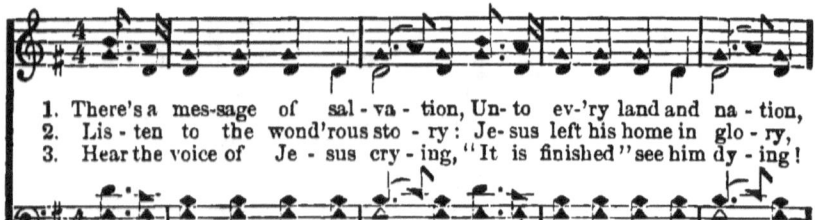

1. There's a mes-sage of sal - va - tion, Un- to ev-'ry land and na - tion,
2. Lis - ten to the wond'rous sto - ry : Je- sus left his home in glo - ry,
3. Hear the voice of Je - sus cry - ing, "It is finished" see him dy - ing !

'Tis so full and free, 'Tis for you and me, And re - cord- ed in his word !
And up - on the tree, Died for you and me, To re-deem a world of woe !
Tho' for sin-ners slain, He a - rose a- gain, In a bright e - ter - nal day !

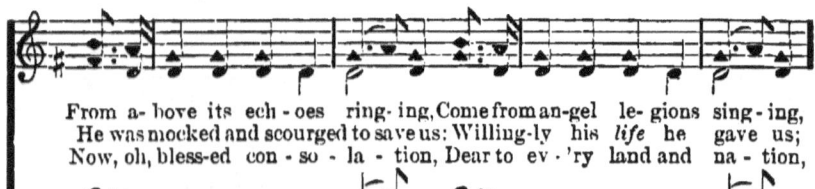

From a- bove its ech - oes ring- ing, Come from an-gel le- gions sing- ing,
He was mocked and scourged to save us: Willing-ly his *life* he gave us;
Now, oh, bless-ed con - so - la - tion, Dear to ev - 'ry land and na - tion,

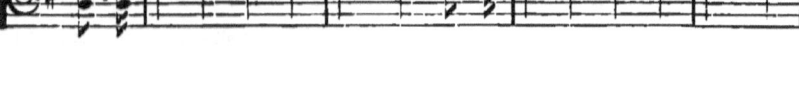

'Tis a glad re-frain, And the sweetest strain Mortal ears have ev - er heard.
From his riv - en side, Came a crim-son tide, That can make us white as snow.
On the Lord be-lieve, And you shall re-ceive Grace to wash all sin a - way.

Copyright, 1889, by Chas. H. Gabriel.

No. 91. BEYOND THE SUNSET.

JOSEPHINE POLLARD.   W. O. PERKINS, by per.

DUET OR SEMI-CHORUS.

1. Be - yond the sunset's radiant glow, There is a brighter world, I know,
2. Be - yond the sunset's pur-ple rim, Beyond the twilight deep and dim,
3. Be - yond this des-ert dark and drear, The gold-en cit - y will ap-pear,
4. Those gold - en portals ev - er shine Beyond the reach of day's de-cline,

Where gold-en glo-ries ev - er shine, Beyond the thought of day's decline.
Where clouds and darkness never come, My soul shall find its heavenly home.
And morning's lovely beams a - rise Up - on my mansion in the skies.
And Je - sus bids my soul pre-pare To gain a hap-py entrance there.

FULL CHORUS.

Beyond the sunset's radiant glow, There is a brighter world I know;
radiant glow,

Repeat pp.

Be - yond the sun-set, I may spend De-light-ful days that never end.

MIGHTY TO SAVE. Concluded.

115

MEET ME THERE. Concluded.

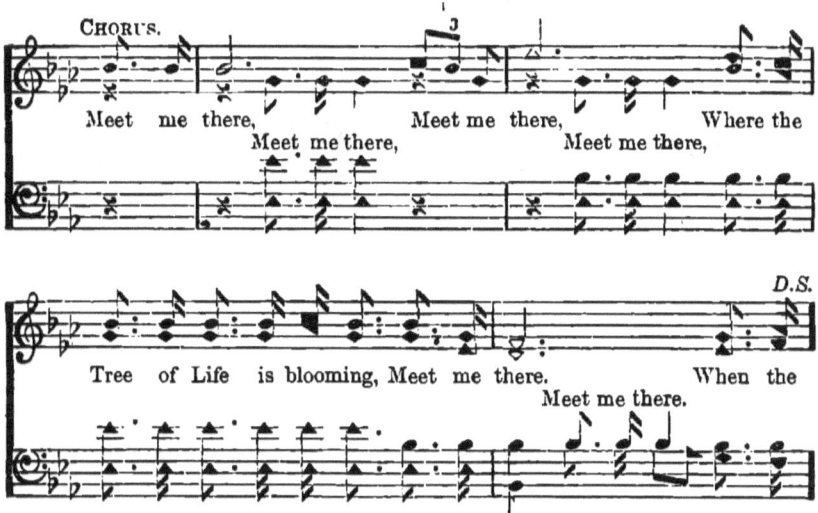

Meet me there, Meet me there, Where the
Meet me there, Meet me there,
Tree of Life is blooming, Meet me there. When the
Meet me there.

No. 98. YARBROUGH.

Miss FRANCES E. HAVERGAL.   Arr. by R. M. McINTOSH.

1 Take my life, and let it be Con-se-crat-ed, Lord, to thee;
2 Take my feet, and let them be Swift and beau-ti-ful for thee;
3 Take my sil-ver and my gold, Not a mite would I with-hold;
4 Take my will and make it thine, It shall be no lon-ger mine;
5 Take my love; my Lord, I pour At thy feet its treas-ure-store;

CHO.—Lord, I give my life to thee, Thine for-ev-er-more to be;

Take my hands, and let them move At the im-pulse of thy love.
Take my voice, and let me sing Al-ways, on-ly for my King.
Take my mo-ments and my days, Let them flow in cease-less praise.
Take my heart, it is thine own, It shall be thy roy-al throne.
Take my-self, and I will be Ev-er, on-ly, all for thee.

Lord, I give my life to thee, Thine for-ev-er-more to be.

By per. R. M. McIntosh.

No. 100. THE JOYFUL PROCLAMATION.

F. M. D.
FRANK M. DAVIS.

1 Send the joy - ful proc - la - ma - tion O'er the mountains, o'er the waves;
2 Send the mes - sage to the dy - ing, He who life e - ter - nal craves,
3 Send the mes - sage o'er the wa - ters, Let it ech - o thro' the caves,

Shout it to the dis - tant na - tions, Bless - ed tid - ings Je - sus saves.
Bid him look in faith to Je - sus, Bless - ed tid - ings Je - sus saves.
Joy - ful news to those in dark - ness, Bless - ed tid - ings Je - sus saves.

CHORUS.

Bless - ed tid - ings, bless - ed tid - ings, Bless - ed
Bless - ed tid - ings, bless - ed tid - ings,

tid - ings Je - sus saves; Bless-ed tid - ings, bless-ed
Bless - ed tid - ings Bless-ed tidings,

tid - ings, Bless- ed tid - ings Je - sus saves.
bless - ed tid - ings, Bless - ed tid - ings Je - sus saves.

Copyright, 1889, by R. M. McIntosh.

We Silently Slumber at Last. Concluded.

slum-ber at last, ... Slum-ber at last. . . . . .
Slum-ber at last, Slumber at last.

No. 102. FATHER OF MERCIES.

F. M. D.   DUET AND CHORUS.   FRANK M. DAVIS.

1 Fa-ther of mercies, I come! Come with my burden to thee, Help other than
2 Fa-ther of mercies, I come! Take then this heart 'tis thine own; Refine it and
3 Fa-ther of mercies, I come! Sweetly to rest in thy love; O take me to

REFRAIN.

thine there is none, Look then in pit - y on me.
make it all pure, Make it thine own royal throne.   } Fa-ther of mer-cies I
dwell Lord with thee, In thine own mansions above.

come, I come, Fa - ther of mer - cies I come, I come.

Copyright, 1889, by R. M. McIntosh.

HANDWRITING ON THE WALL. Concluded.

No. 104. O, LEAD ME TO JESUS.

FRANK M. DAVIS.

1. O, lead me to Jesus, I'm tired of my sin, I'm weary of fighting pollution within; In mercy, now lead me where I may find peace, And where all my sorrows shall cease.
2. O, lead me to Jesus, I know he is love; To save erring children, he came from above; He surely will heal me and pardon my sin, Will comfort my longing within.
3. O, lead me to Jesus, O, show me the way, My soul in its blindness has wandered astray; Then take me to Jesus, so precious as he, The Saviour who suffered for me.

CHORUS.
O, lead me to Jesus, my Saviour and King; O, lead me to Saviour, my Saviour and King; O, lead me, yes, lead me to Jesus, to Jesus my Saviour and King; O, lead me, yes, lead me to

Copyright, 1889, by R. M. McIntosh.

O, LEAD ME TO JESUS. Concluded.

No. 105. ZION. 8s, 7s & 4s.
Dr. Thos. Hastings.

1 { On the mountain's top ap-pear-ing, Lo, the sa-cred her-ald stands,
Wel-come news to Zi-on bear-ing, Zi-on long in hos-tile lands: }

Verse.

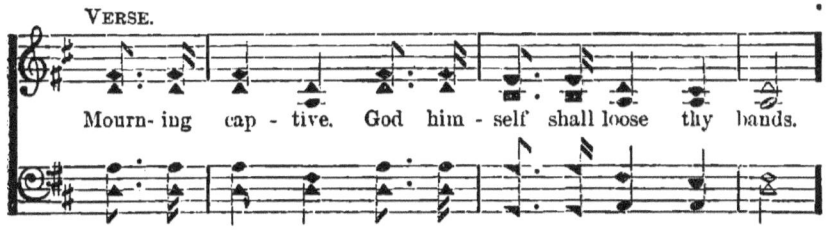

Mourn-ing cap-tive. God him-self shall loose thy bands.

Chorus.

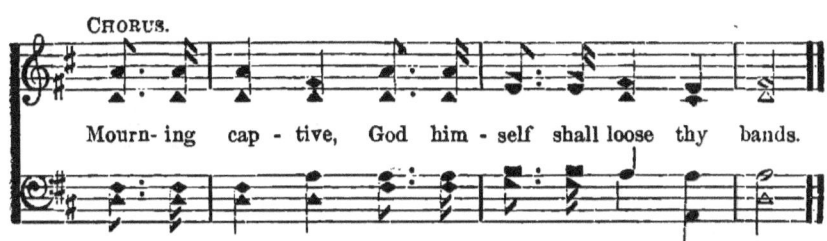

Mourn-ing cap-tive, God him-self shall loose thy bands.

2 Has thy night been long and mournful,
All thy friends unfaithful proved?
Have thy foes been proud and scornful,
By thy sighs and tears unmoved?
　Cease thy mourning,
Zion still is well beloved.

3 God, thy God, will now restore thee!
He himself appears thy friend:
All thy foes shall flee before thee,
Here their boasts and triumphs end:
　Great deliverance,
Zion's King vouchsafes to send.

JESUS IS PASSING TO-DAY. Concluded.

ritard ad libitum.

sin-ner receive him, re-ceive him; He's pass-ing, yes passing to-day.

No. 107. HAPPY DAY. L. M.

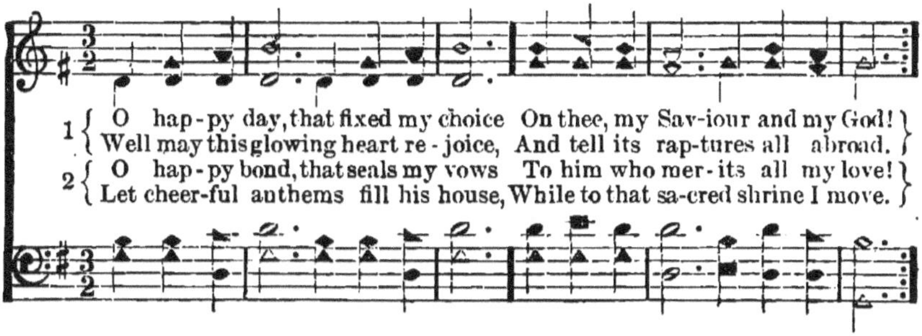

1. { O hap-py day, that fixed my choice On thee, my Sav-iour and my God! }
   { Well may this glowing heart re-joice, And tell its rap-tures all abroad. }
2. { O hap-py bond, that seals my vows To him who mer-its all my love! }
   { Let cheer-ful anthems fill his house, While to that sa-cred shrine I move. }

CHORUS. *FINE.*

Hap-py day, hap-py day, When Je-sus washed my sins a-way.

D.S.

He taught me how to watch and pray, And live re-joic-ing ev-'ry day:

3 'Tis done: the great transaction's done!
  I am my Lord's, and he is mine;
  He drew me, and I followed on.
  Charmed to confess the voice divine.

4 High Heaven, that heard the solemn vow,
  That vow renewed shall daily hear,
  Till in life's latest hour I bow,
  And bless in death a bond so dear.

No. 108 PRAISE THE LORD.

Mrs. M. B. C. Slade.   Dr. A. B. Everett.

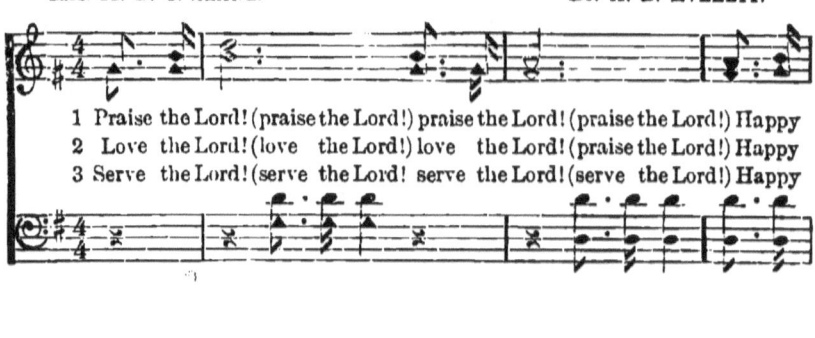

1 Praise the Lord! (praise the Lord!) praise the Lord! (praise the Lord!) Happy
2 Love the Lord! (love the Lord!) love the Lord! (praise the Lord!) Happy
3 Serve the Lord! (serve the Lord! serve the Lord! (serve the Lord!) Happy

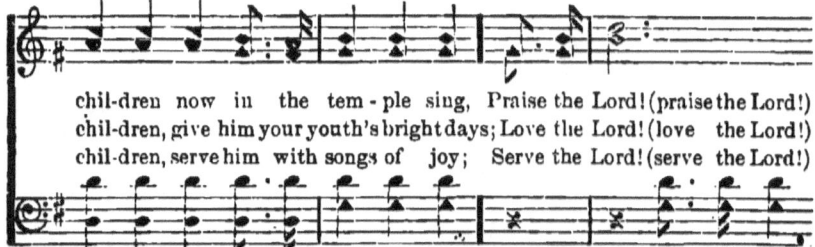

chil-dren now in the tem-ple sing, Praise the Lord! (praise the Lord!)
chil-dren, give him your youth's bright days; Love the Lord! (love the Lord!)
chil-dren, serve him with songs of joy; Serve the Lord! (serve the Lord!)

praise the Lord! Ho-san-na to the Lord our King. O praise him for the
love the Lord! He ev-er lov-eth you, he says. O love him, for he
serve the Lord! And let his work your hands employ. O serve him, what-so-

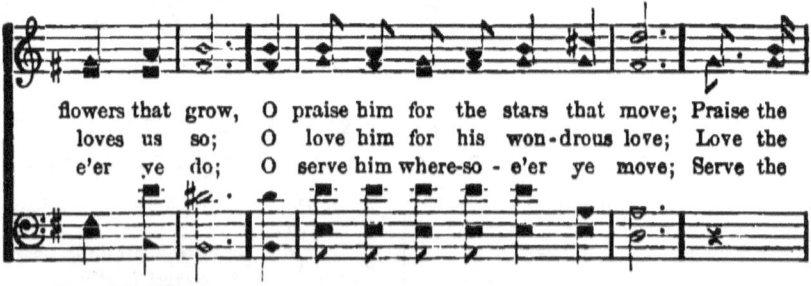

flowers that grow, O praise him for the stars that move; Praise the
loves us so;   O love him for his won-drous love; Love the
e'er ye do;   O serve him where-so-e'er ye move; Serve the

By per. R. M. McIntosh.

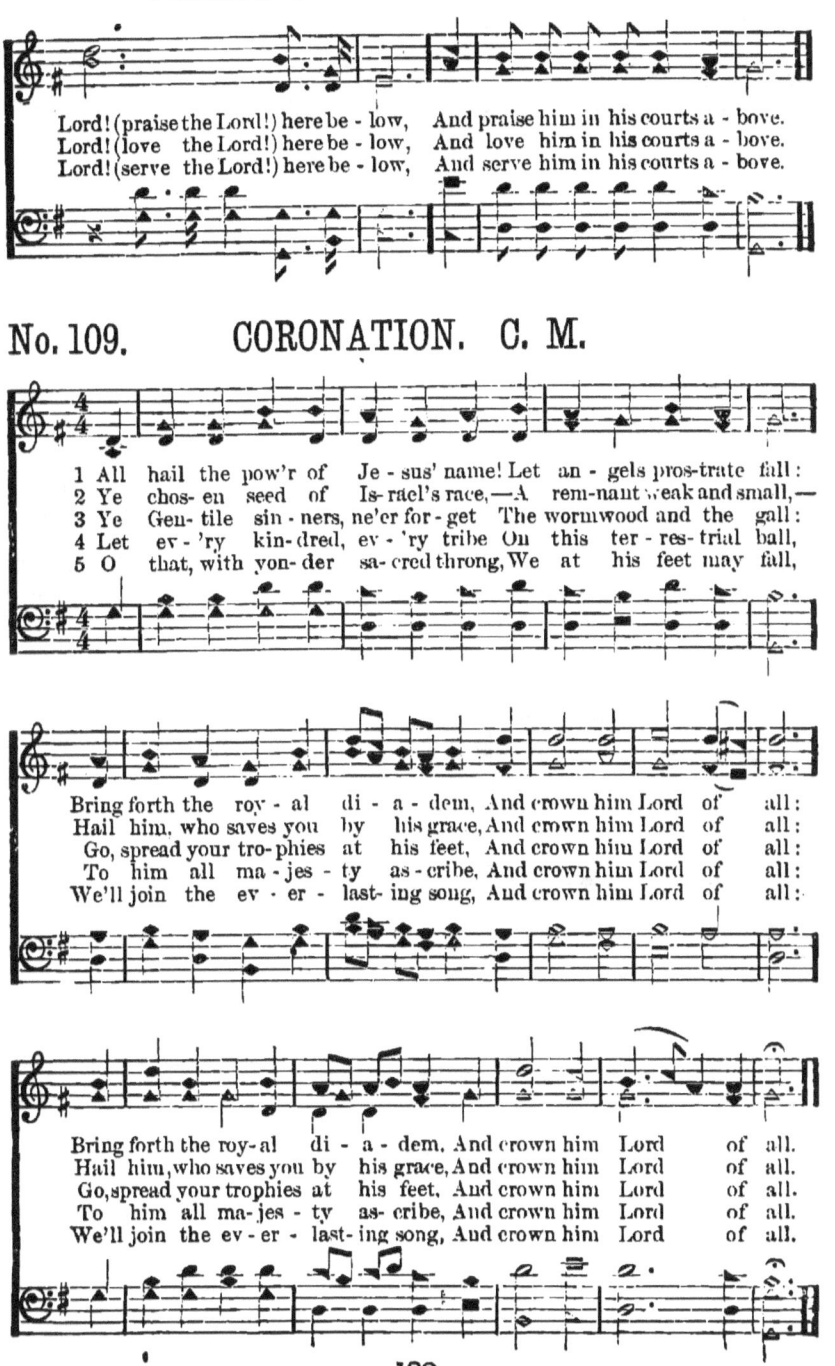

God Wants the Boys and Girls. Concluded.

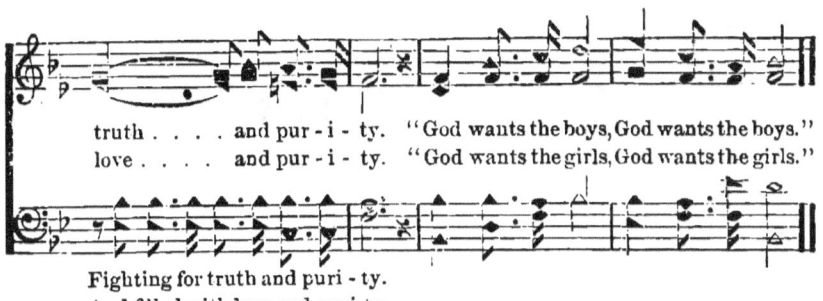

truth .... and pur-i-ty. "God wants the boys, God wants the boys."
love .... and pur-i-ty. "God wants the girls, God wants the girls."

Fighting for truth and puri-ty.
And filled with love and puri-ty.

No. 111. GREGORY.

L. C. EVERETT, by per.

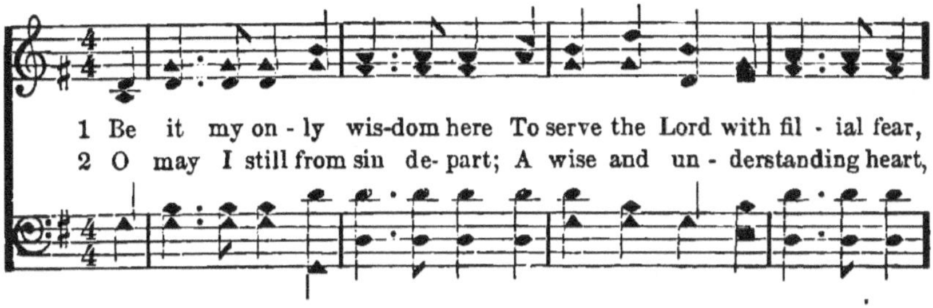

1 Be it my on-ly wis-dom here To serve the Lord with fil-ial fear,
2 O may I still from sin de-part; A wise and un-derstanding heart,

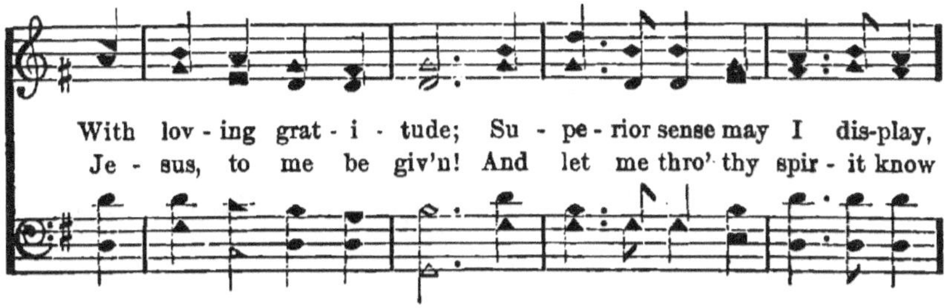

With lov-ing grat-i-tude; Su-pe-rior sense may I dis-play,
Je-sus, to me be giv'n! And let me thro' thy spir-it know

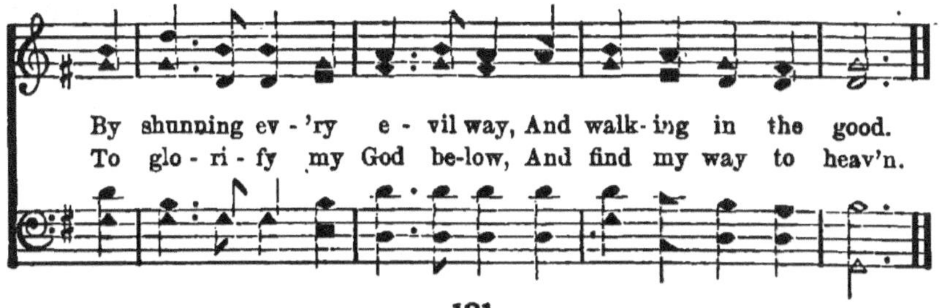

By shunning ev-'ry e-vil way, And walk-ing in the good.
To glo-ri-fy my God be-low, And find my way to heav'n.

Gather Around the Christmas Tree. Concluded.

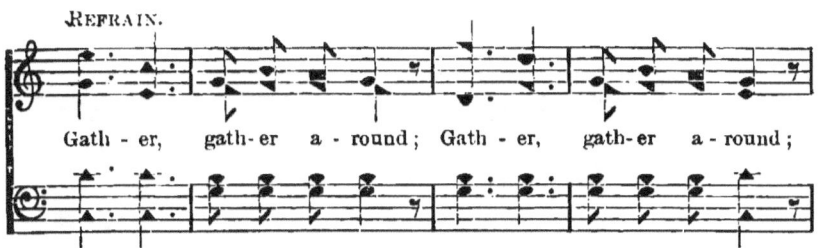

Gath - er, gath - er a - round; Gath - er, gath- er a - round;

Gath - er, gath - er a - round, Gath - er a - round the tree.

No. 113.   LABAN. S. M.

GEO. HEATH.   Dr. L. MASON.

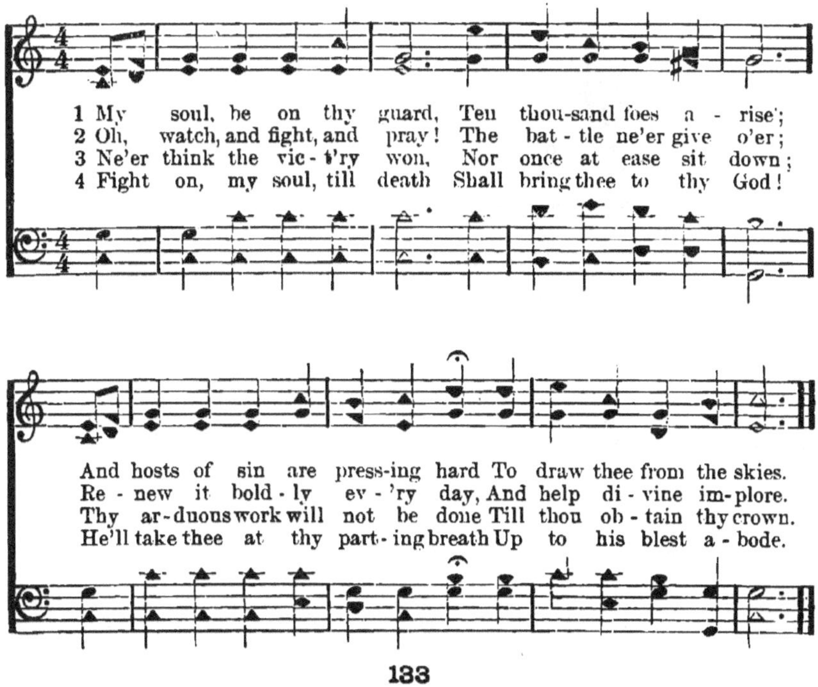

1 My soul, be on thy guard, Ten thou-sand foes a - rise;
2 Oh, watch, and fight, and pray! The bat - tle ne'er give o'er;
3 Ne'er think the vic - t'ry won, Nor once at ease sit down;
4 Fight on, my soul, till death Shall bring thee to thy God!

And hosts of sin are press-ing hard To draw thee from the skies.
Re - new it bold - ly ev - 'ry day, And help di - vine im-plore.
Thy ar - duous work will not be done Till thou ob - tain thy crown.
He'll take thee at thy part - ing breath Up to his blest a - bode.

WE ARE COMING. Concluded.

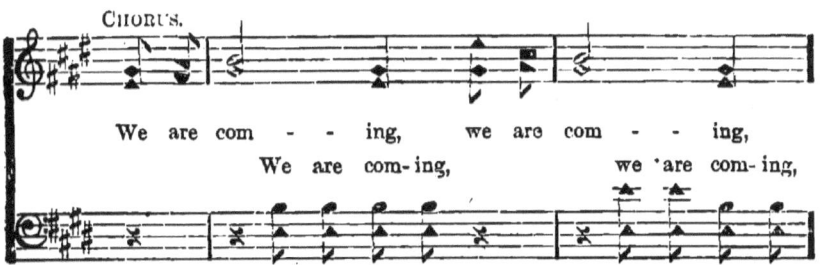

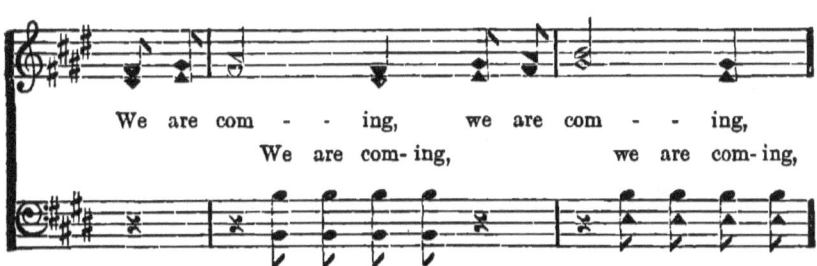

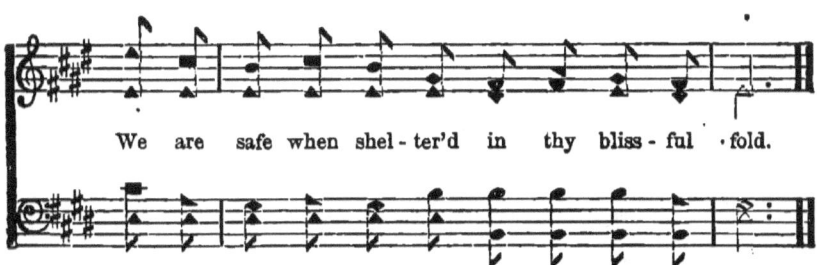

No. 118. SCATTER BRIGHT SMILES.

G. W. L. G. W. LYON, by per.

1 Scat - ter bright smiles all a - round you, They cheer like the
2 Scat - ter bright smiles all a - round you, More pre-cious than
3 Scat - ter bright smiles all a - round you, Re - mem - ber the
4 Scat - ter bright smiles all a - round you, We nev - er know

beau - ti - ful rain, That falls on the with - er - ing flow - ers, And
treas-ures of gold, They light-en the bur-dens of oth - ers, They
weak and op - press'd, O, smile on the poor and the need - y, And
where they may fall, Then ev - er be read - y and will - ing, To

CHORUS.

makes them bloom sweetly a - gain.
cheer up the young and the old.
com - fort the sad and dis - tress'd.
scat - ter bright smiles o - ver all.

Then scatter bright smiles, they will

nev - er be lost, Re-mem-ber your mission be - low; Scatter bright smiles,

scatter bright smiles, Wher - ev - er, wher - ev - er you go.

BLESSED IS HE. Concluded.

- dur- eth tem-p-ta - tion, Bless-ed is he, bless-ed is he.

No. 120. FOR THEE, OH, SINLESS EDEN!

Mrs. ESTELLE OLTROGGE.   Mrs. ESTELLE OLTROGGE.

1 For thee, oh, sin-less E - den, My heart doth ev - er sigh;
2 Oh, why do sin-sick mor - tals Still cling to earth's al - loy,
3 I'll seek this heav'nly coun - try, And with my lat - est breath

For flow- ers ev - er fade - less, That bloom and nev - er die.
When just with- in the por - tals Of E - den there is joy?
I'll praise our lov - ing Sav - iour, Who saved my soul from death.

Oh! coun- try of for - give - ness, Oh! land with-out a tear,
Un - told, and nev - er end - ing, With Je - sus ev - er near,
And then from sin de - liv - ered, I'll rise to joys un - known,

Where grief gives place to glad - ness, And love reigns with-out fear.
And an - gel voi - ces blend - ing With those of Kin-dred dear?
For - ev - er and for - ev - er, To wor-ship at His throne.

Copyright, 1889, by R. M. McIntosh.

No. 121. CALLING FOR YOU.

MARY SPARKS WHEELER. LEONARD DAUGHERTY.

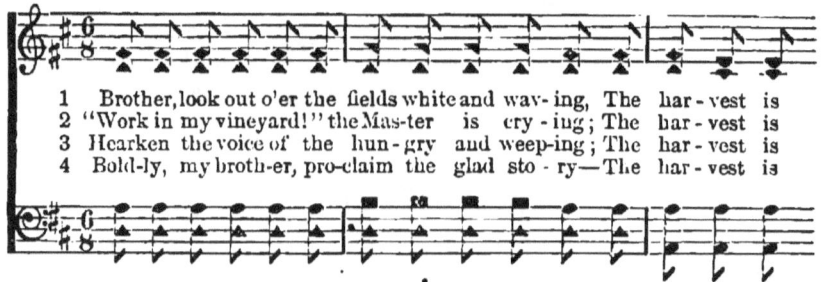

1 Brother, look out o'er the fields white and wav-ing; The har-vest is
2 "Work in my vineyard!" the Mas-ter is cry-ing; The har-vest is
3 Hearken the voice of the hun-gry and weep-ing; The har-vest is
4 Bold-ly, my broth-er, pro-claim the glad sto-ry—The har-vest is

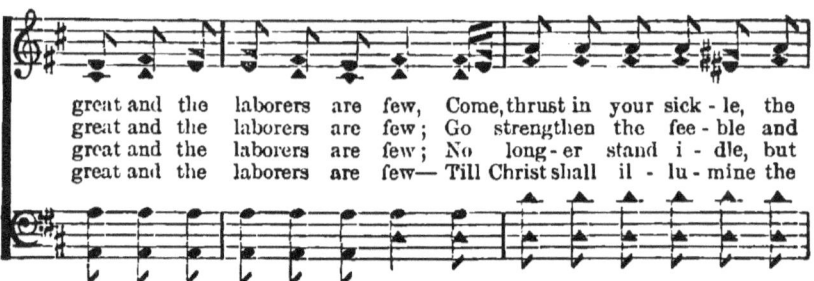

great and the laborers are few, Come, thrust in your sick-le, the
great and the laborers are few; Go strengthen the fee-ble and
great and the laborers are few; No long-er stand i-dle, but
great and the laborers are few— Till Christ shall il-lu-mine the

ripened grain saving, The Lord of the har-vest is call-ing for you!
comfort the dy-ing, The Lord of the har-vest is call-ing for you.
en-ter the reaping, The Lord of the har-vest is call-ing for you.
earth with his glo-ry, The Lord of the har-vest is call-ing for you.

Call - - ing for you, ... Call - - - ing for
CHORUS.
Call-ing, Call-ing for you, Calling,

Copyright, 1889, by R. M. McIntosh.

CALLING FOR YOU. Concluded.

you, . . .
Call-ing for you, The Lord of the har-vest is call-ing for you;
Call - - ing for you, ... Call - - ing for
Call-ing, Call-ing for you, Call-ing,
you, . . .
Call-ing for you, The Lord of the har-vest is call-ing for you.

No. 122. ROSS. C. M.

Dr. A. B. EVERETT, by per.

1 By faith we find the place a-bove, The Rock that rent in twain,
2 Je-sus, to thy dear wounds we flee; We sink in-to thy side;

Beneath the shade of dy-ing love, And in the cleft re-main.
Assured that all who trust in thee Shall ev-er-more a-bide.

No. 123 NEARER HOME.

F. M. DAVIS. A. J. SHOWALTER.

1 Ev-'ry day brings us near-er to the bet-ter land, Near-er
2 Ev-'ry day brings us near-er to the land of love, Near-er
3 Ev-'ry day brings us near-er to the pearl-y gates, Near-er

home, (Near-er home,) near-er home, (near-er home,) Ev-'ry
home, (Near-er home,) near-er home, (near-er home,) Ev-'ry
home, (Near-er home,) near-er home, (near-er home,) Ev-'ry

day brings us near-er to the Lord's right hand, Near-er
day brings us near-er to the fields a-bove, Near-er
day brings us near-er where the Sav-iour waits, Near-er

home, (Near-er home,) near-er home, (near-er home,) We will
home, (Near-er home,) near-er home, (near-er home,) Oh, the
home, (Near-er home,) near-er home, (near-er home,) Oh, the

sing and re-joice while the days are quick-ly pass-ing, Ev-er
way oft-en-times may seem lone-ly, dark, and drear-y, And our
joy we shall know when we reach the land im-mor-tal, And have

Copyright, 1887, by E. O. Excell.

NEARER HOME. Concluded.

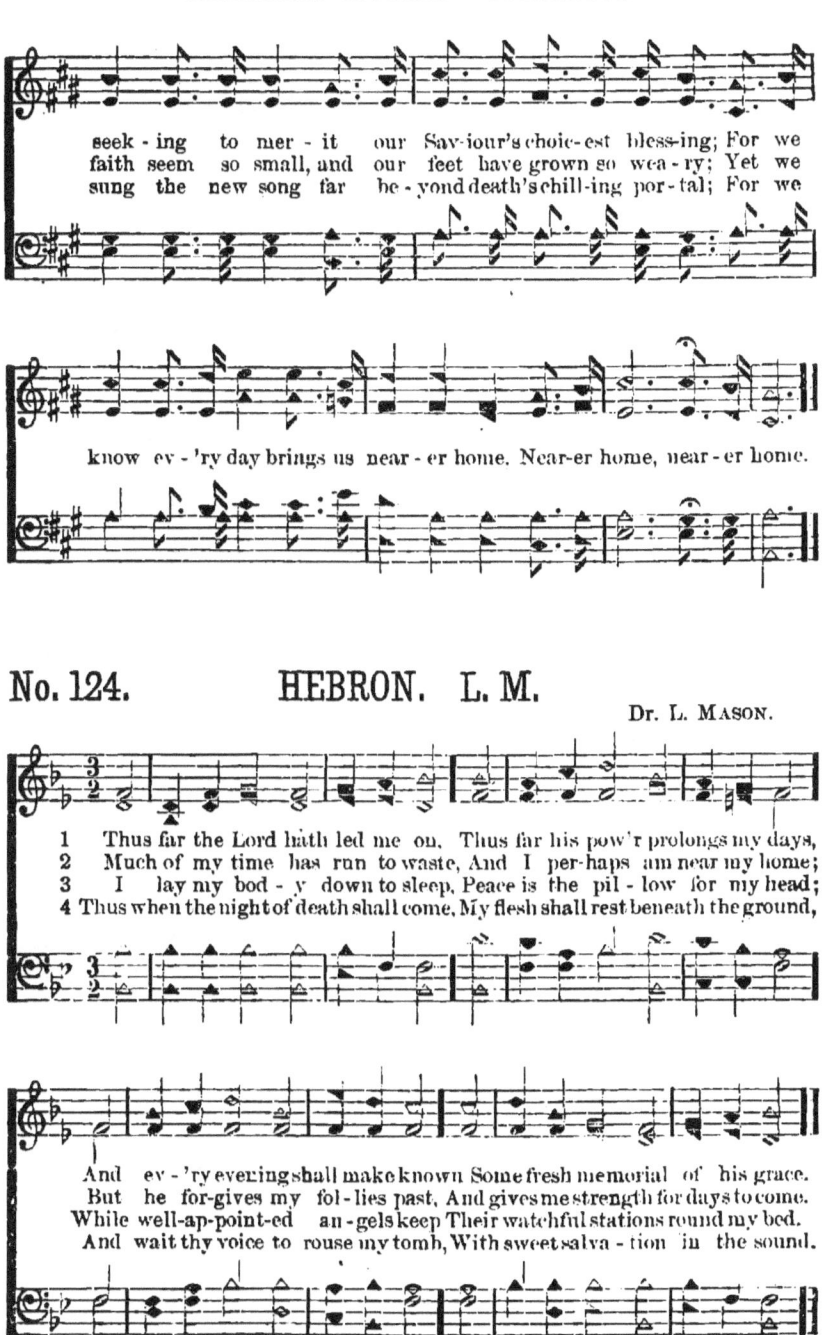

seek - ing to mer - it our Sav-iour's choic-est bless-ing; For we
faith seem so small, and our feet have grown so wea - ry; Yet we
sung the new song far be - yond death's chill-ing por - tal; For we

know ev - 'ry day brings us near - er home. Near-er home, near - er home.

No. 124. HEBRON. L. M.
Dr. L. Mason.

1 Thus far the Lord hath led me on, Thus far his pow'r prolongs my days,
2 Much of my time has run to waste, And I per-haps am near my home;
3 I lay my bod - y down to sleep, Peace is the pil - low for my head;
4 Thus when the night of death shall come, My flesh shall rest beneath the ground,

And ev - 'ry evening shall make known Some fresh memorial of his grace.
But he for-gives my fol - lies past, And gives me strength for days to come.
While well-ap-point-ed an - gels keep Their watchful stations round my bed.
And wait thy voice to rouse my tomb, With sweet salva - tion in the sound.

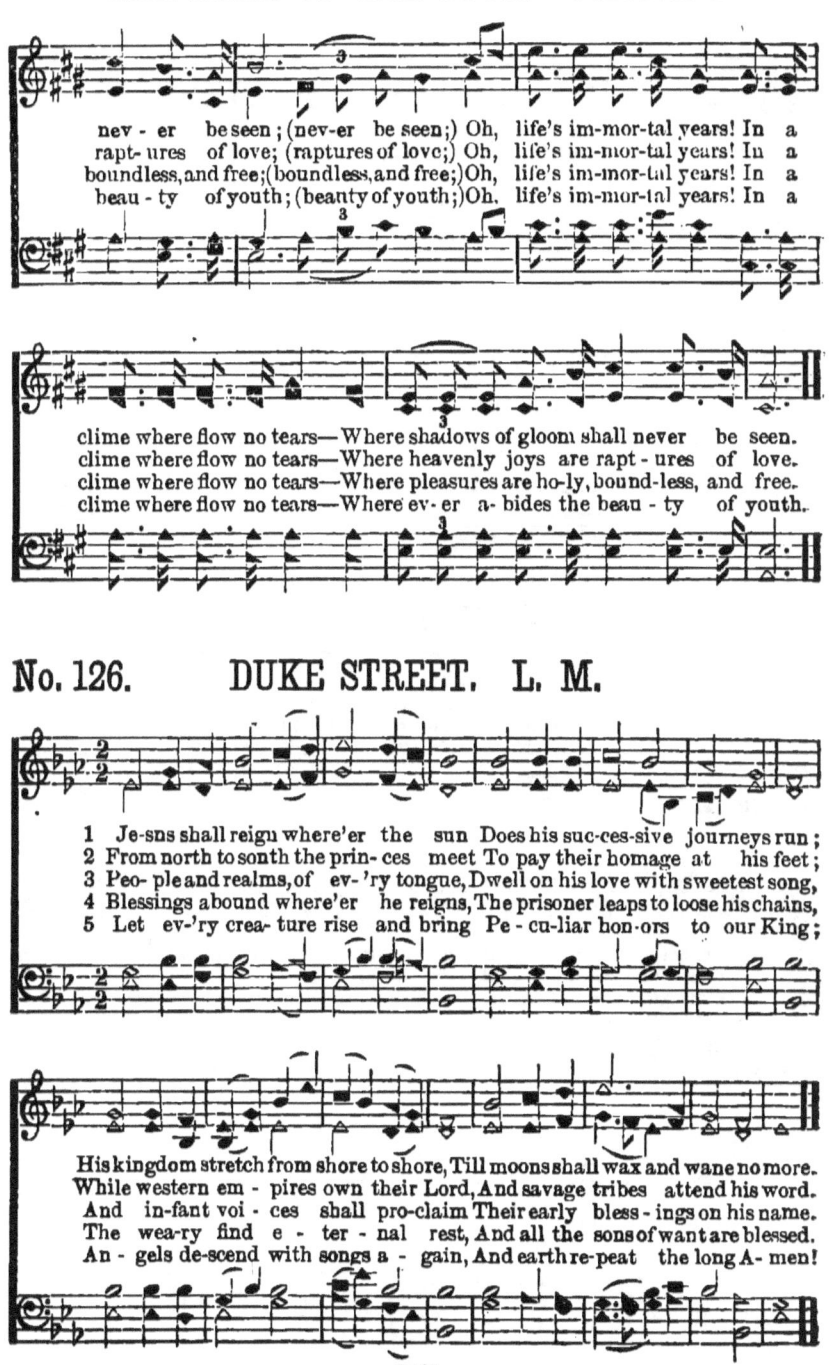

Drifting Toward the Golden Shore. Concluded.

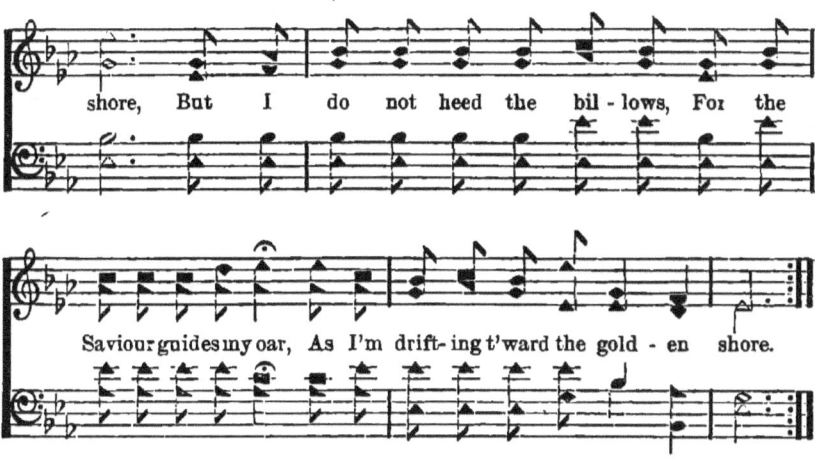

shore, But I do not heed the bil-lows, For the Saviour guides my oar, As I'm drift-ing t'ward the gold-en shore.

No. 128. MARTYN. 7s. Double.

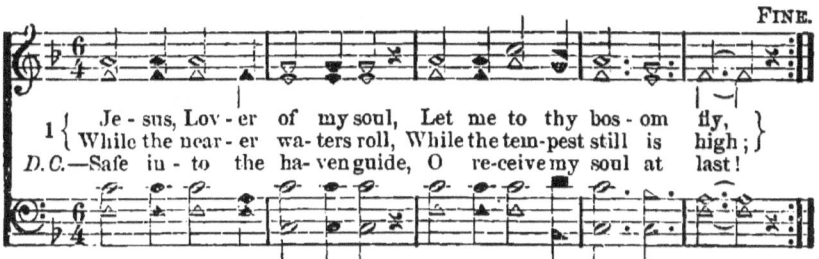

1 { Je-sus, Lov-er of my soul, Let me to thy bos-om fly, }
  { While the near-er wa-ters roll, While the tem-pest still is high; }
D.C.—Safe in-to the ha-ven guide, O re-ceive my soul at last!

Hide me. O my Sav-iour, hide, Till the storm of life be past;

2 Other refuge have I none,
  Hangs my helpless soul on thee:
  Leave, ah! leave me not alone.
  Still support and comfort me!
  All my trust on thee is stayed.
  All my help from thee I bring.
  Cover my defenceless head
  With the shadow of thy wing.

3 Thou. O Christ, art all I want:
  More than all in thee I find:
  Raise the fallen, cheer the faint,
  Heal the sick, and lead the blind;

Just and holy is thy name;
I am all unrighteousness:
False, and full of sin, I am;
Thou art full of truth and grace

4 Plenteous grace with thee is found
  Grace to cover all my sin:
  Let the healing streams abound,
  Make and keep me pure within:
  Thou of life the fountain art;
  Freely let me take of thee:
  Spring thou up within my heart,
  Rise to all eternity!

BECAUSE HE FIRST LOVED ME. Concluded.

No. 130. BOYLSTON. S. M.

Dr. L. Mason.

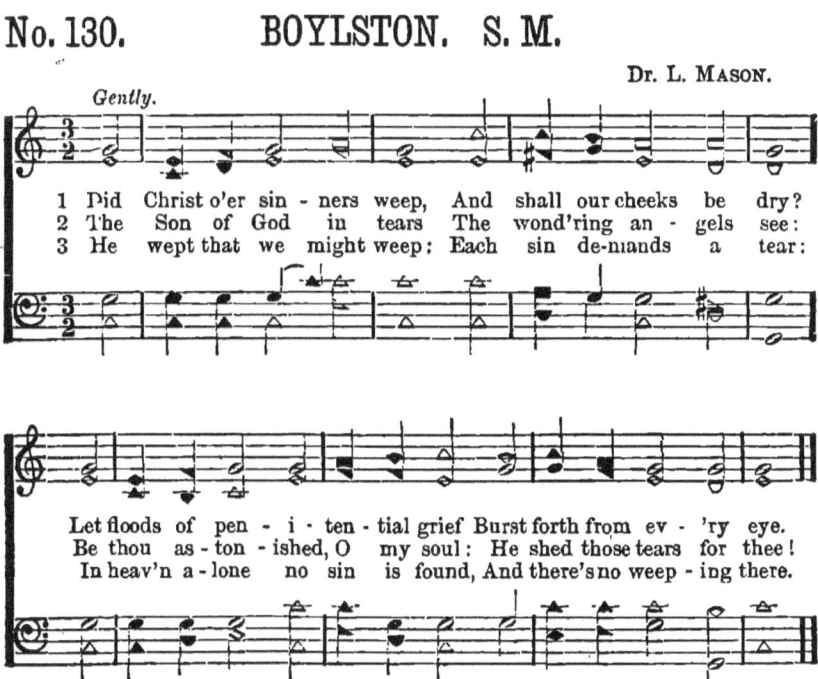

1 Did Christ o'er sin-ners weep, And shall our cheeks be dry?
2 The Son of God in tears The wond'ring an-gels see:
3 He wept that we might weep: Each sin de-mands a tear:

Let floods of pen-i-ten-tial grief Burst forth from ev-'ry eye.
Be thou as-ton-ished, O my soul: He shed those tears for thee!
In heav'n a-lone no sin is found, And there's no weep-ing there.

AS PANTS THE HEART. Concluded.

for cooling streams, . . . So pants my soul, ... O Lord, for thee.
for cooling streams, So pants my soul, so pants my soul, O Lord, for thee.

No. 132.   HOME. C. M. Double.

R. M. McIntosh, by per.

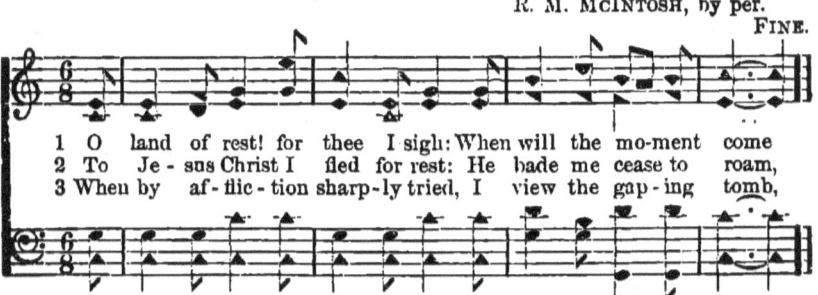

1 O land of rest! for thee I sigh: When will the mo-ment come
2 To Je - sus Christ I fled for rest: He bade me cease to roam,
3 When by af-flic-tion sharp-ly tried, I view the gap-ing tomb,

D. C.—This world's a wil-der-ness of woe—This world is not my home.
But, ah! my pass-port was not seal'd—I could not yet go home.
I long to quit th' unhallow'd ground, And dwell with Christ at home.

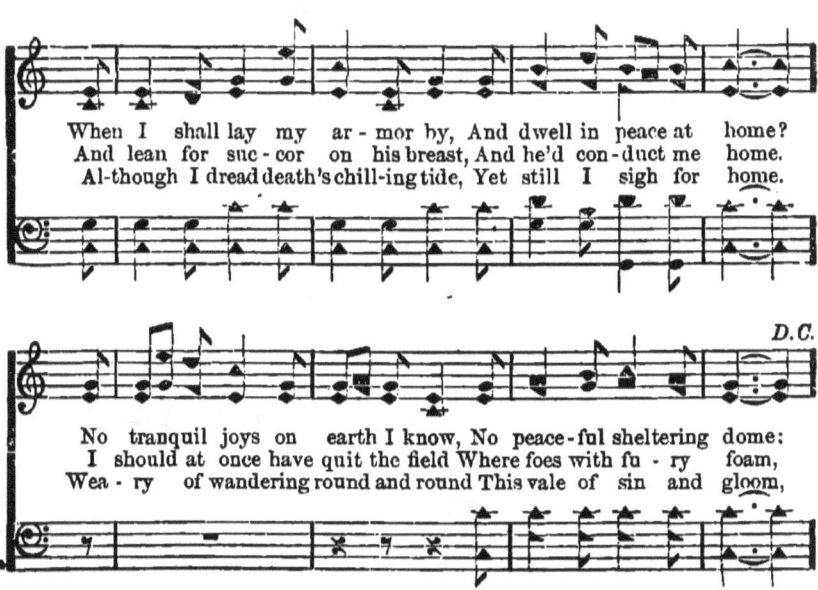

When I shall lay my ar-mor by, And dwell in peace at home?
And lean for suc-cor on his breast, And he'd con-duct me home.
Al-though I dread death's chill-ing tide, Yet still I sigh for home.

No tranquil joys on earth I know, No peace-ful sheltering dome:
I should at once have quit the field Where foes with fu - ry foam,
Wea - ry of wandering round and round This vale of sin and gloom,

As We've Sown So Shall We Reap. Concluded.

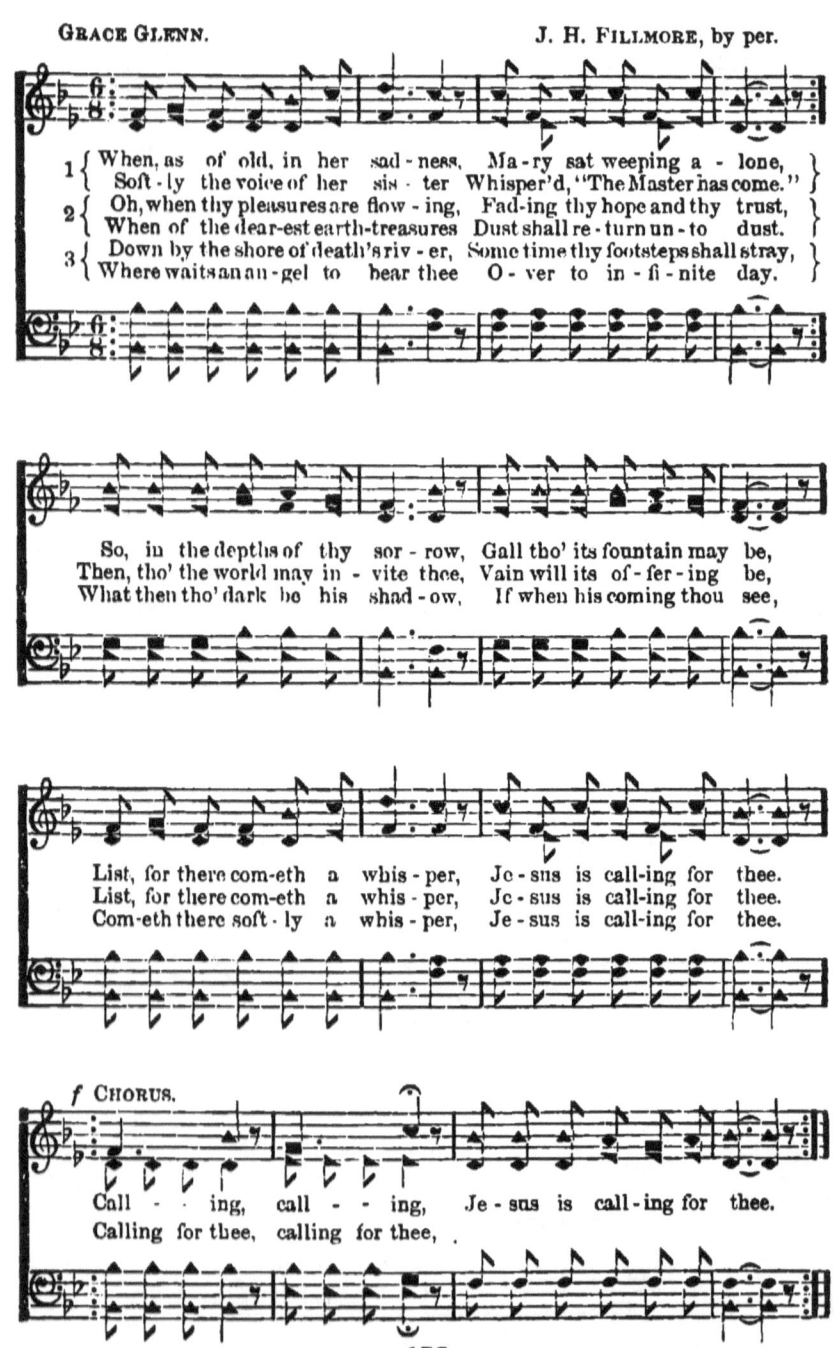

No. 135   NEARER TO THEE.

JESSIE H. BROWN.   J. H. FILLMORE, by per.
SOLO.

1 Back from the Long A - go, Dis - tant and dim, Breath-ing a
2 Oft in an hour of bliss Comes the re - frain, Bid - ding me
3 Thus let me dai - ly rise Near - er thy throne, Near - er the

warn - ing low, Comes a sweet hymn; Fraught with my childhood dreams,
find in this, Heav - en - ly gain; E'en in my griefs I say:
last - ing prize Kept for thine own; E'en when Death's her - alds come,

Slower.

It is for me; Sa - cred and ten-der seems, "Near - er to thee;"—
Fa - ther I flee Ont of this cloud-ed way, "Near - er to thee;"—
Lord, may they be An - gels to lead me home, "Near - er to thee;"—

CHORUS. *Tempo.*

"Still all my song shall be, Near - er, my God, to thee,
"So by my woes to be Near - er, my God, to thee,
"An - gels to beck - on me, Near - er, my God, to thee,

Near - er, my God, to thee, Near - er to thee."

Copyright, 1887, by Fillmore Bros.

What a Gathering That will be. Concluded.

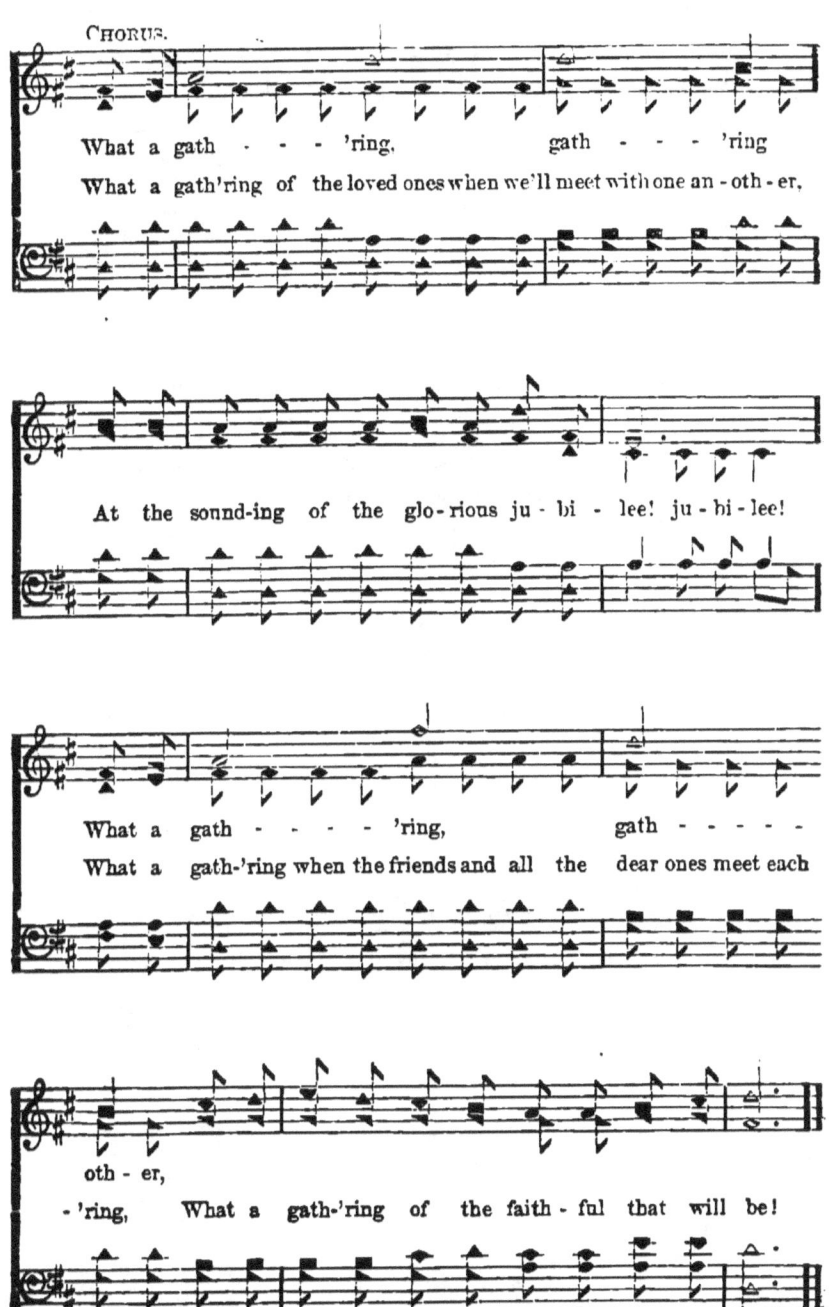

159

No. 137. CLEAVE TO THE SAVIOUR.

Rev. J. H. MARTIN, D. D. R. M. McINTOSH.

1 Would you please and hon-or Je-sus? Follow him in all you do;
2 Would you have a friend in Je-sus, To sup-port you in your way?
3 Do you long to be with Je-sus, And a crown of life se-cure?

Would you win his love and fa-vor? Be his serv-ant, faithful, true.
Own him as your Lord and Master, Him re-ceive, and love, o-bey.
Be thou pa-tient in his service, Meekly to the end en-dure.

REFRAIN.

Cleave to the Sav-iour day by day, Tempted by sin, go seek him in pray'r; Du-ty per-form, and courage dis-play, Cleave to the Sav-iour ev-'ry-where.

Copyright, 1885, by R. M. McIntosh.

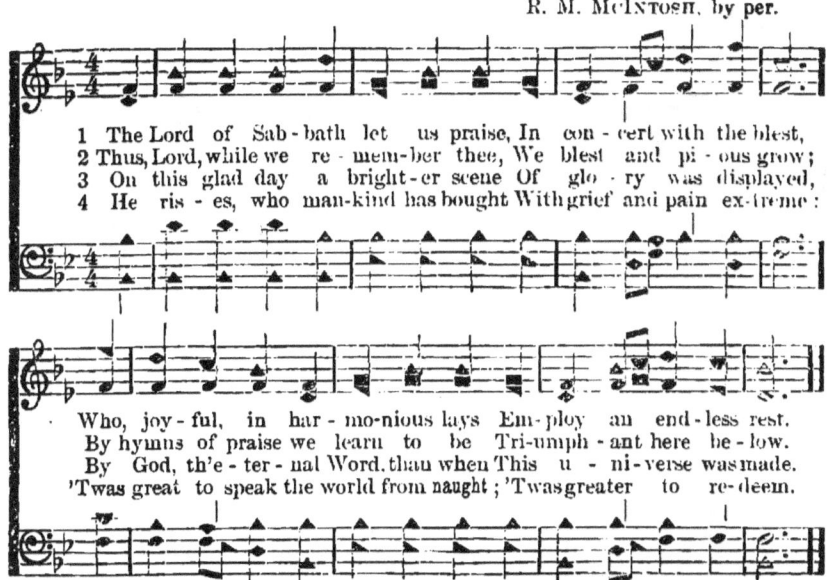

R. M. McIntosh, by per.

1 The Lord of Sab-bath let us praise, In con-cert with the blest,
2 Thus, Lord, while we re-mem-ber thee, We blest and pi-ous grow;
3 On this glad day a bright-er scene Of glo-ry was displayed,
4 He ris-es, who man-kind has bought With grief and pain ex-treme:

Who, joy-ful, in har-mo-nious lays Em-ploy an end-less rest.
By hymns of praise we learn to be Tri-umph-ant here be-low.
By God, th'e-ter-nal Word, than when This u-ni-verse was made.
'Twas great to speak the world from naught; 'Twas greater to re-deem.

No. 139. VAUGHAN. C. M.

R. M. McIntosh, by per.

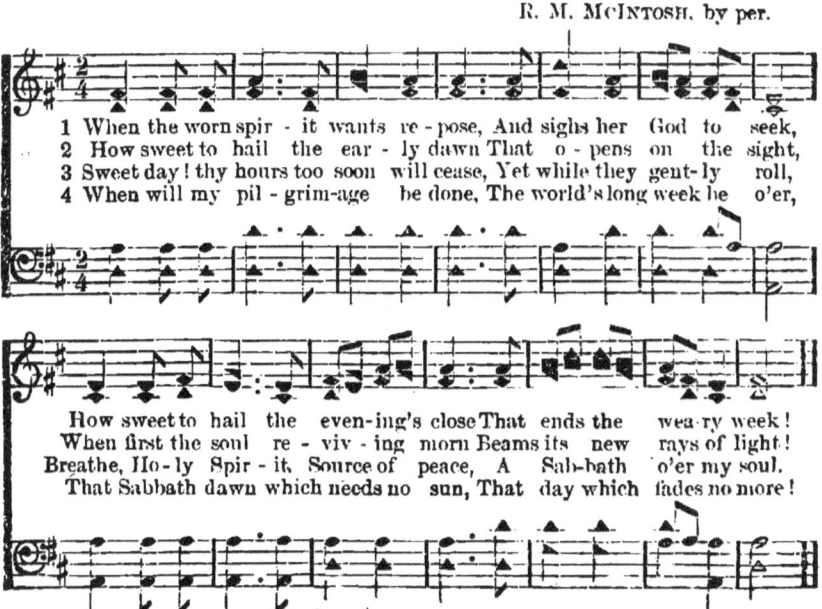

1 When the worn spir-it wants re-pose, And sighs her God to seek,
2 How sweet to hail the ear-ly dawn That o-pens on the sight,
3 Sweet day! thy hours too soon will cease, Yet while they gent-ly roll,
4 When will my pil-grim-age be done, The world's long week be o'er,

How sweet to hail the even-ing's close That ends the wea-ry week!
When first the soul re-viv-ing morn Beams its new rays of light!
Breathe, Ho-ly Spir-it, Source of peace, A Sab-bath o'er my soul.
That Sabbath dawn which needs no sun, That day which fades no more!

161

No. 140. SUMMERS. L. M.

R. M. McIntosh, by per.

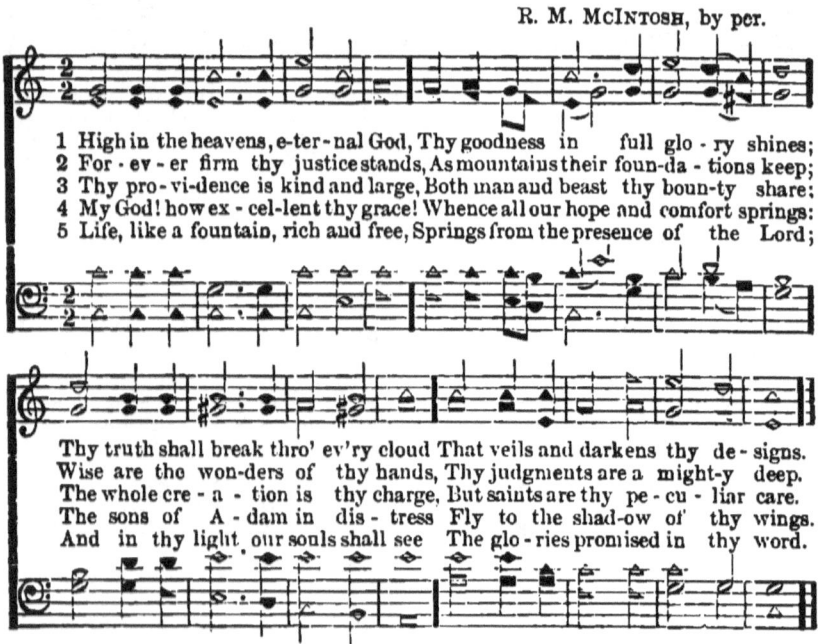

1 High in the heavens, e-ter-nal God, Thy goodness in full glo-ry shines;
2 For-ev-er firm thy justice stands, As mountains their foun-da-tions keep;
3 Thy pro-vi-dence is kind and large, Both man and beast thy boun-ty share;
4 My God! how ex-cel-lent thy grace! Whence all our hope and comfort springs;
5 Life, like a fountain, rich and free, Springs from the presence of the Lord;

Thy truth shall break thro' ev'ry cloud That veils and darkens thy de-signs.
Wise are the won-ders of thy hands, Thy judgments are a might-y deep.
The whole cre-a-tion is thy charge, But saints are thy pe-cu-liar care.
The sons of A-dam in dis-tress Fly to the shad-ow of thy wings.
And in thy light our souls shall see The glo-ries promised in thy word.

No. 141. BROKER. L. M.

R. M. McIntosh, by per.

Softly, gently, yet distinct.

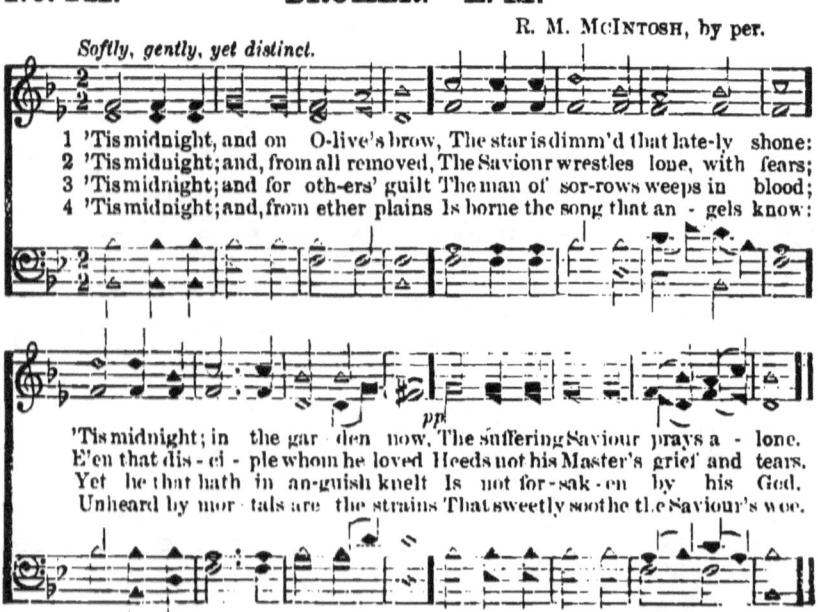

1 'Tis midnight, and on O-live's brow, The star is dimm'd that late-ly shone;
2 'Tis midnight; and, from all removed, The Saviour wrestles lone, with fears;
3 'Tis midnight; and for oth-ers' guilt The man of sor-rows weeps in blood;
4 'Tis midnight; and, from ether plains Is borne the song that an-gels know;

'Tis midnight; in the gar-den now, The suffering Saviour prays a-lone.
E'en that dis-ci-ple whom he loved Heeds not his Master's grief and tears.
Yet he that hath in an-guish knelt Is not for-sak-en by his God.
Unheard by mor-tals are the strains That sweetly soothe the Saviour's woe.

No. 142. VIRGINIA. C. M.

N. E. EVERETT, by per.

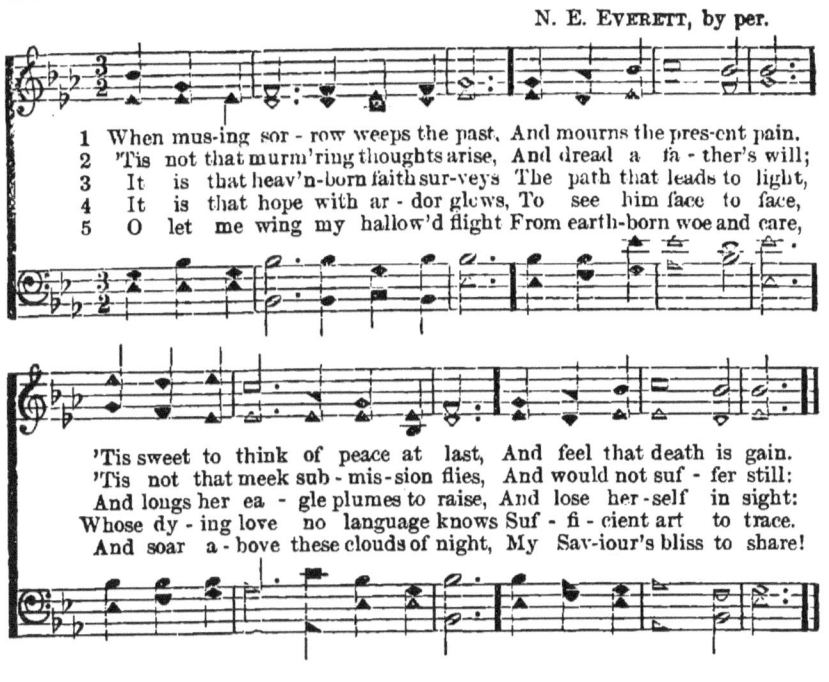

1 When mus-ing sor - row weeps the past, And mourns the pres-ent pain.
2 'Tis not that murm'ring thoughts arise, And dread a fa - ther's will;
3 It is that heav'n-born faith sur-veys The path that leads to light,
4 It is that hope with ar - dor glows, To see him face to face,
5 O let me wing my hallow'd flight From earth-born woe and care,

'Tis sweet to think of peace at last, And feel that death is gain.
'Tis not that meek sub - mis-sion flies, And would not suf - fer still:
And longs her ea - gle plumes to raise, And lose her-self in sight:
Whose dy - ing love no language knows Suf - fi - cient art to trace.
And soar a - bove these clouds of night, My Sav-iour's bliss to share!

No. 143. KAVANAUGH. L. M.

R. M. McINTOSH, by per.

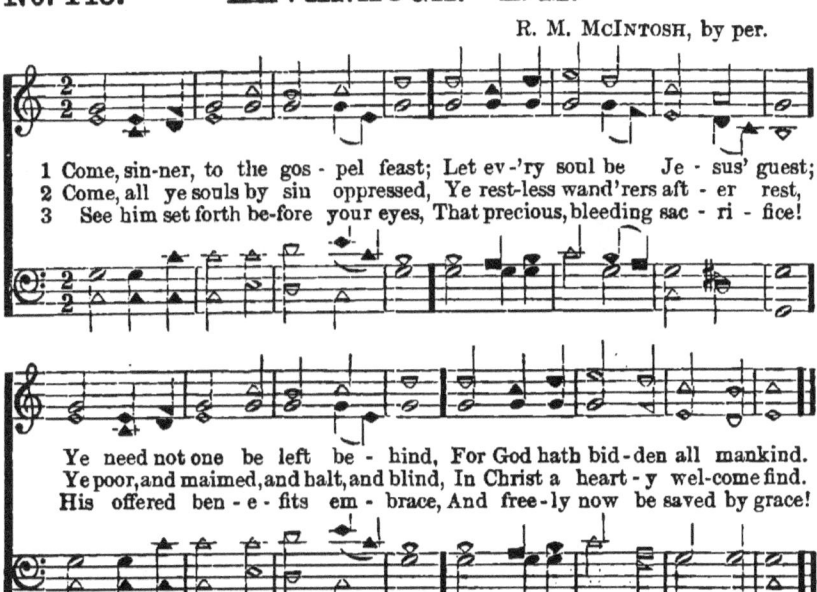

1 Come, sin-ner, to the gos - pel feast; Let ev-'ry soul be Je - sus' guest;
2 Come, all ye souls by sin oppressed, Ye rest-less wand'rers aft - er rest,
3 See him set forth be-fore your eyes, That precious, bleeding sac - ri - fice!

Ye need not one be left be - hind, For God hath bid-den all mankind.
Ye poor, and maimed, and halt, and blind, In Christ a heart - y wel-come find.
His offered ben - e - fits em - brace, And free-ly now be saved by grace!

No. 144.   MOULTON. S. M.

L. C. CHISHOLM, by per.

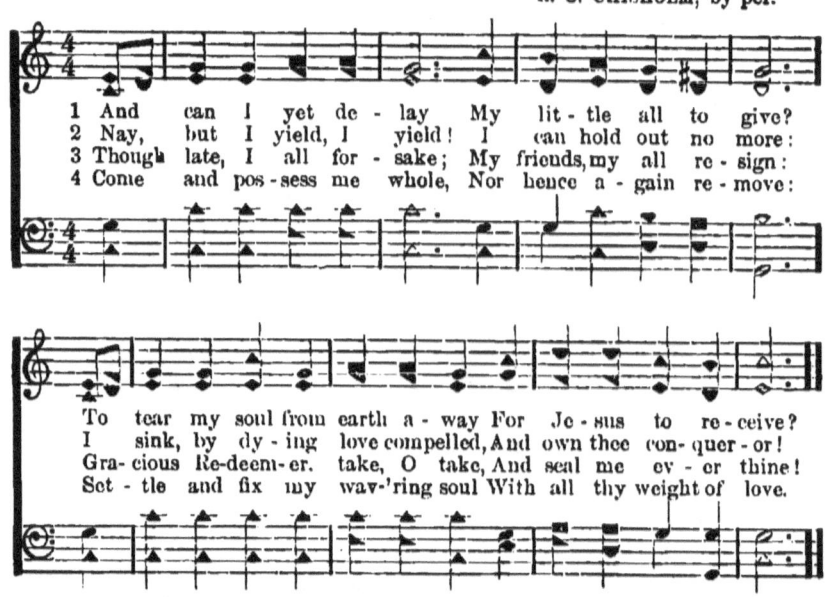

1 And can I yet de-lay My lit-tle all to give?
2 Nay, but I yield, I yield! I can hold out no more:
3 Though late, I all for-sake; My friends, my all re-sign:
4 Come and pos-sess me whole, Nor hence a-gain re-move:

To tear my soul from earth a-way For Je-sus to re-ceive?
I sink, by dy-ing love compelled, And own thee con-quer-or!
Gra-cious Re-deem-er, take, O take, And seal me ev-er thine!
Set-tle and fix my wav-'ring soul With all thy weight of love.

No. 145.   SOLITUDE. C. M.

L. C. EVERETT, by per.

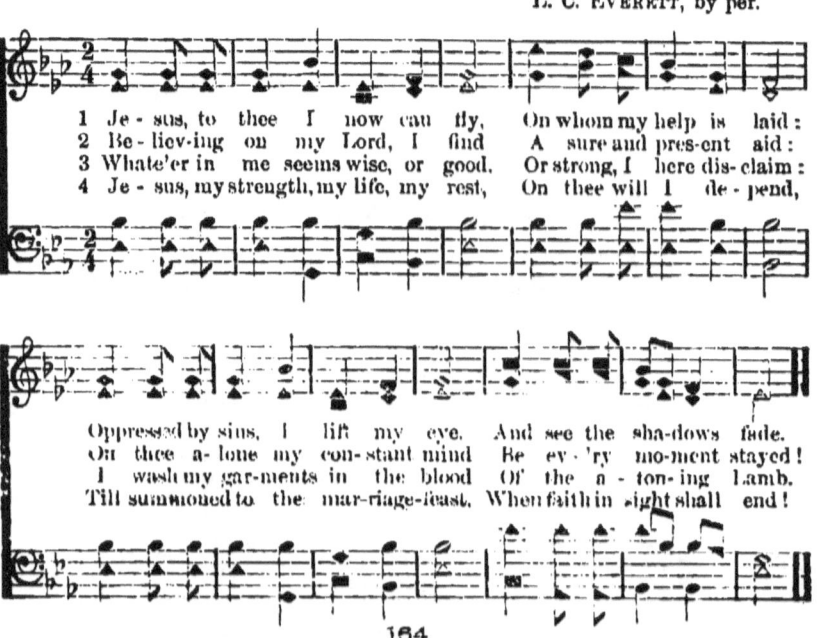

1 Je-sus, to thee I now can fly, On whom my help is laid:
2 Be-liev-ing on my Lord, I find A sure and pres-ent aid:
3 Whate'er in me seems wise, or good, Or strong, I here dis-claim:
4 Je-sus, my strength, my life, my rest, On thee will I de-pend,

Oppressed by sins, I lift my eye, And see the sha-dows fade.
On thee a-lone my con-stant mind Be ev-'ry mo-ment stayed!
I wash my gar-ments in the blood Of the a-ton-ing Lamb.
Till summoned to the mar-riage-feast, When faith in sight shall end!

L. C. EVERETT, by per.

1 Fa-ther, I stretch my hands to thee, No oth-er help I know;
2 What did thine on-ly Son en-dure, Be-fore I drew my breath!
3 Au-thor of faith, to thee I lift My wea-ry, long-ing eyes:
4 Sure-ly thou canst not let me die: O speak, and I shall live;
5 The worst of sin-ners would re-joice, Could they but see thy face:

If thou with-draw thy-self from me, Ah! whith-er shall I go?
What pain, what la-bor to se-cure My soul from end-less death!
O let me now re-ceive that gift, My soul with-out it dies!
And here I will un-wear-ied lie, Till thou thy Spir-it give.
O let me hear thy quick'ning voice, And taste thy pard'ning grace!

No. 147. PAUL. S. M.

L. C. EVERETT, by per.

1 Je-sus, the Con-qu'ror, reigns, In glo-rious strength ar-rayed,
2 Ye sons of men, re-joice In Je-sus' might-y love:
3 Ex-tol his king-ly pow'r; Kiss the ex-alt-ed Son,
4 Our Ad-vo-cate with God, He un-der-takes our cause,

His kingdom o-ver all maintains, And bids the earth be glad!
Lift up your heart, lift up your voice, To him who rules a-bove.
Who died, and lives to die no more, High on his Fa-ther's throne:
And spreads thro' all the earth a-broad The vic-t'ry of his cross.

FARMVILLE. Concluded.

O Lamb of God, I come! O Lamb of God, I come!

2 Just as I am—and waiting not
To rid my soul of one dark blot, [spot;
To thee, whose blood can cleanse each
O Lamb of God, I come!

3 Just as I am—though tossed about
With many a conflict, many a doubt,
With fears within and wars without—
O Lamb of God, I come!

4 Just as I am—poor, wretched, blind:
Sight, riches, healing of the mind,
Yea, all I need, in thee to find,
O Lamb of God, I come!

5 Just as I am—thy love unknown
Has broken every barrier down:
Now to be thine, yea, thine alone,
O Lamb of God, I come!

No. 150. SCHUMANN. S. M.
L. C. EVERETT, by per.

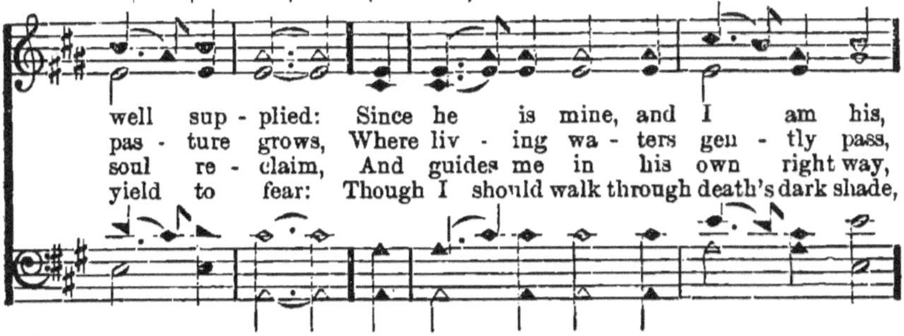

1 The Lord my Shep-herd is, I shall be well sup-plied: Since he is mine, and I am his, What can I want be-side? And full sal-va-tion flows, What can I want be-side? And full sal-va-tion flows.

2 He leads me to the place Where heaven-ly pas-ture grows, Where liv-ing wa-ters gen-tly pass, For his most ho-ly name, For his most ho-ly name.

3 If e'er I go a-stray, He doth my soul re-claim, And guides me in his own right way, My Shepherd's with me there. My Shepherd's with me there.

4 While he af-fords his aid, I can-not yield to fear: Though I should walk through death's dark shade,

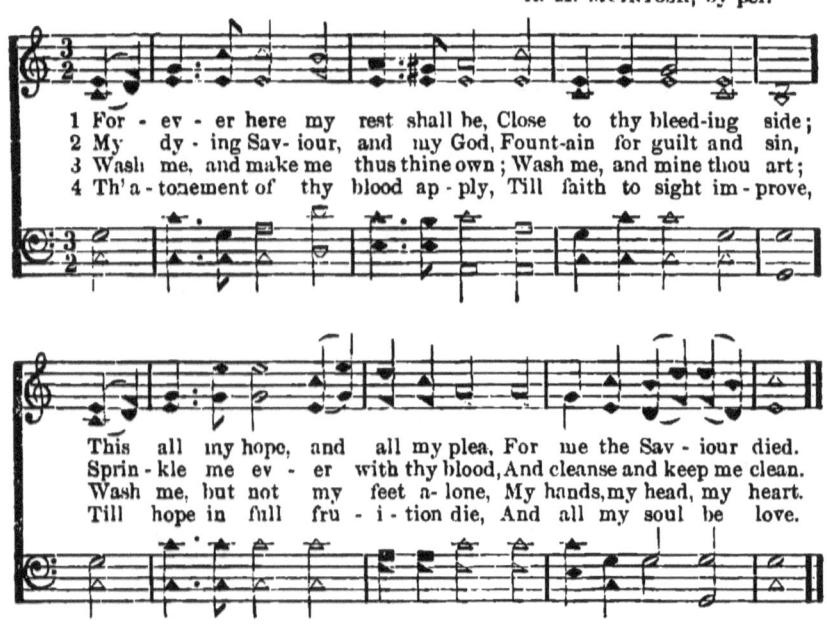

1 For-ev-er here my rest shall be, Close to thy bleed-ing side;
2 My dy-ing Sav-iour, and my God, Fount-ain for guilt and sin,
3 Wash me, and make me thus thine own; Wash me, and mine thou art;
4 Th' a-tonement of thy blood ap-ply, Till faith to sight im-prove,

This all my hope, and all my plea, For me the Sav-iour died.
Sprin-kle me ev-er with thy blood, And cleanse and keep me clean.
Wash me, but not my feet a-lone, My hands, my head, my heart.
Till hope in full fru-i-tion die, And all my soul be love.

No. 152.   KERLIN. C. M.

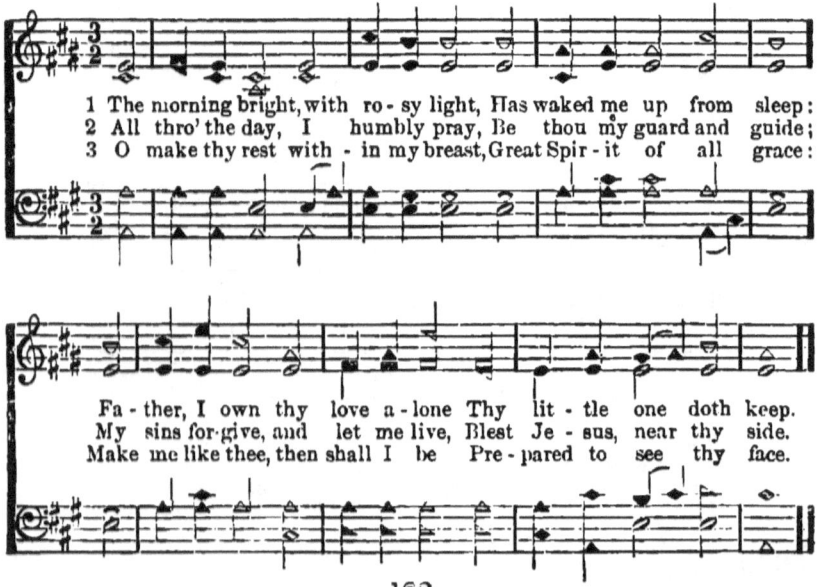

1 The morning bright, with ro-sy light, Has waked me up from sleep:
2 All thro' the day, I humbly pray, Be thou my guard and guide;
3 O make thy rest with-in my breast, Great Spir-it of all grace:

Fa-ther, I own thy love a-lone Thy lit-tle one doth keep.
My sins for-give, and let me live, Blest Je-sus, near thy side.
Make me like thee, then shall I be Pre-pared to see thy face.

R. M. McIntosh, by per.

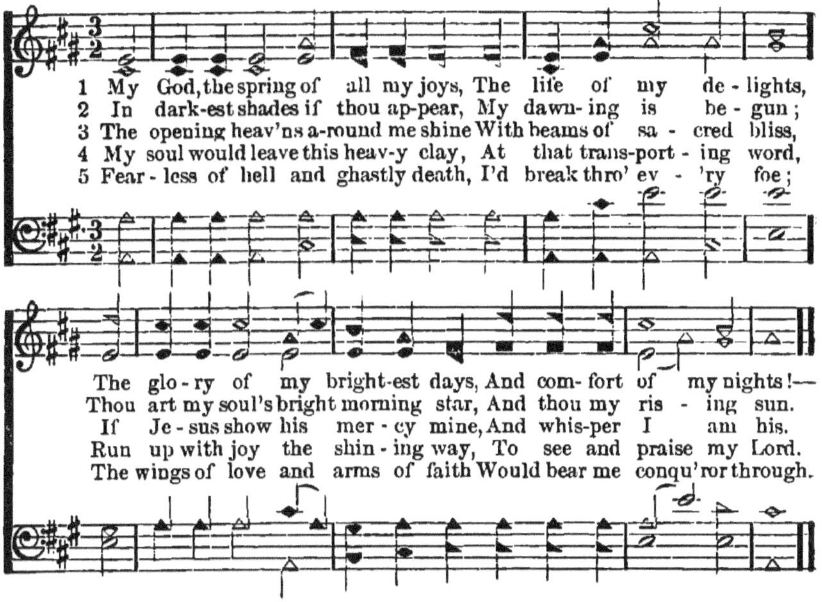

1. My God, the spring of all my joys, The life of my de-lights,
   The glo-ry of my bright-est days, And com-fort of my nights!—
2. In dark-est shades if thou ap-pear, My dawn-ing is be-gun;
   Thou art my soul's bright morning star, And thou my ris-ing sun.
3. The opening heav'ns a-round me shine With beams of sa-cred bliss,
   If Je-sus show his mer-cy mine, And whis-per I am his.
4. My soul would leave this heav-y clay, At that trans-port-ing word,
   Run up with joy the shin-ing way, To see and praise my Lord.
5. Fear-less of hell and ghastly death, I'd break thro' ev-'ry foe;
   The wings of love and arms of faith Would bear me conqu'ror through.

No. 154. GILL. 8s, 7s & 4s. (8th P. M.)

R. M. McIntosh, by per.

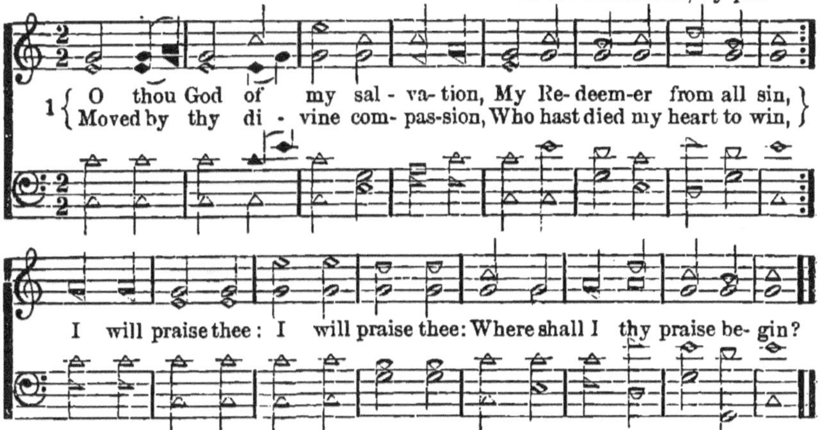

1. { O thou God of my sal-va-tion, My Re-deem-er from all sin,
     Moved by thy di-vine com-pas-sion, Who hast died my heart to win, }
   I will praise thee: I will praise thee: Where shall I thy praise be-gin?

2. Though unseen, I love the Saviour:
   He hath brought salvation near—
   Manifests his pardoning favor,
   And, when Jesus doth appear,
   Soul and body
   Shall his glorious image bear.

3. While the angel choirs are crying,
   Glory to the great I AM!
   I with them will still be vying,
   Glory! glory to the Lamb!
   O how precious
   Is the sound of Jesus' name!

4. Angels now are hovering round us,
   Unperceived they mix the throng,
   Wondering at the love that crowned us,
   Glad to join the holy song:
   Hallelujah!
   Love and praise to Christ belong!

No. 157. McCOY. S. M.

L. C. EVERETT, by per.

1 Come, Ho-ly Spir-it, come, With en-er-gy Di-vine,
2 O melt this fro-zen heart; This stub-born will sub-due;
3 The prof-it will be mine, But thine shall be the praise:

And on this poor be-night-ed soul, With beams of mer-cy shine.
Each e-vil pas-sion o-ver-come, And form me all a-new!
And un-to thee will I de-vote The rem-nant of my days.

No. 158. GEORGIA. S. M.

R. M. McINTOSH, by per.

1 Be-hold th'a-maz-ing sight, The Sav-iour lift-ed high:
2 For whom, for whom, my heart, Were all these sor-rows borne?
3 For love of us he bled, And all in tor-ture died:
4 I see, and I a-dore In sym-pa-thy of love:

Be-hold the Son of God's de-light Ex-pire in ag-o-ny.
Why did he feel that piercing smart, And meet that va-rious scorn?
'Twas love that bowed his faint-ing head, And oped his gush-ing side.
I feel the strong, at-trac-tive power, To lift my soul a-bove.

No. 159. BONNELL. C. M.

R. M. McIntosh, by per.

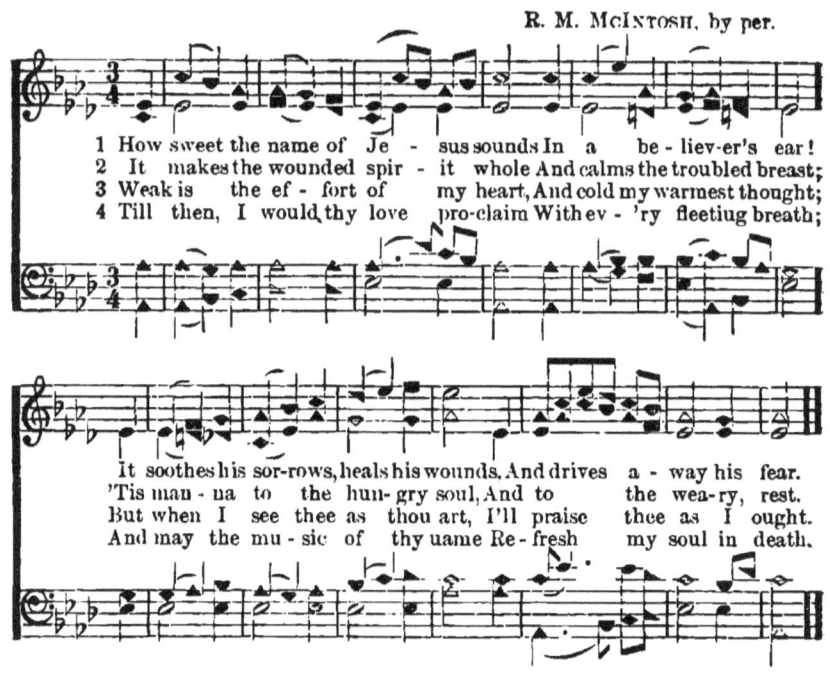

1 How sweet the name of Jesus sounds In a believer's ear!
It soothes his sorrows, heals his wounds, And drives away his fear.
2 It makes the wounded spirit whole And calms the troubled breast;
'Tis manna to the hungry soul, And to the weary, rest.
3 Weak is the effort of my heart, And cold my warmest thought;
But when I see thee as thou art, I'll praise thee as I ought.
4 Till then, I would thy love proclaim With ev-'ry fleeting breath;
And may the music of thy name Refresh my soul in death.

No. 160. ASHVILLE. C. M.

Dr. A. B. Everett, by per.

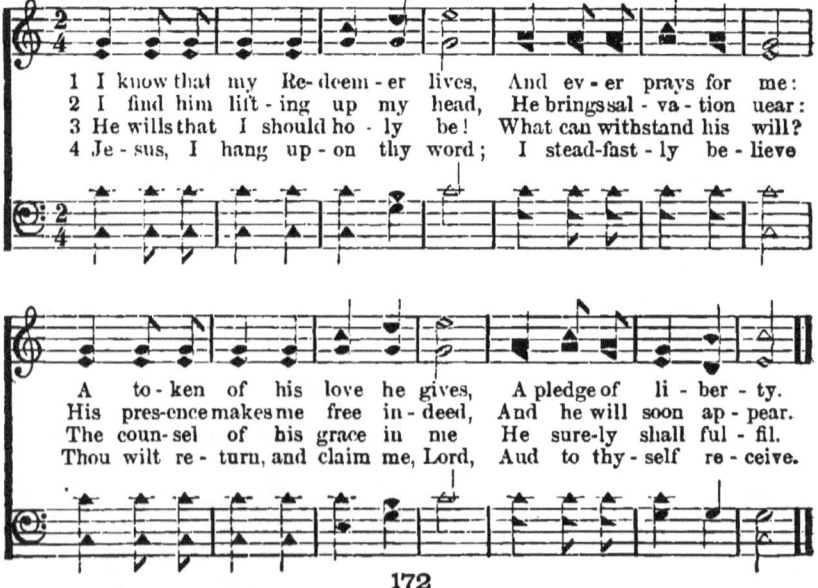

1 I know that my Redeemer lives, And ever prays for me:
A token of his love he gives, A pledge of liberty.
2 I find him lifting up my head, He brings salvation near:
His presence makes me free indeed, And he will soon appear.
3 He wills that I should holy be! What can withstand his will?
The counsel of his grace in me He surely shall fulfil.
4 Jesus, I hang upon thy word; I steadfastly believe
Thou wilt return, and claim me, Lord, And to thyself receive.

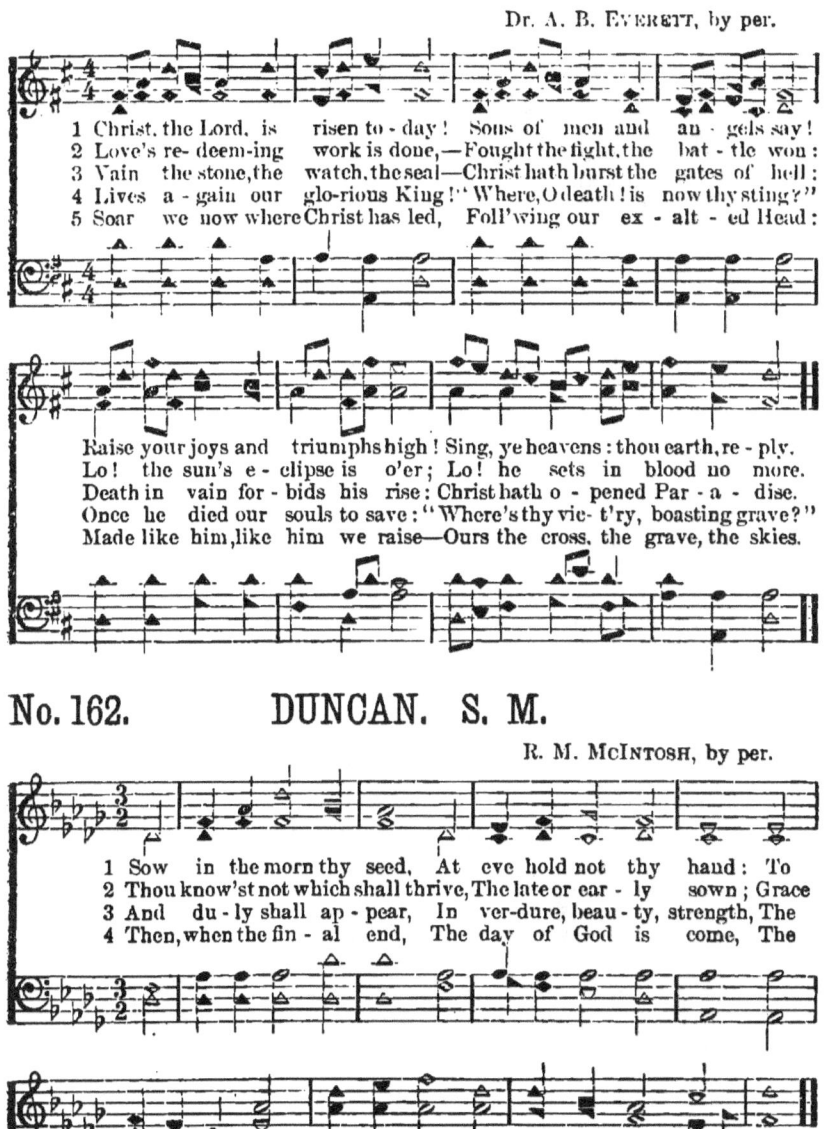

No. 163. PUMROY. 7s.

L. C. EVERETT, by per.

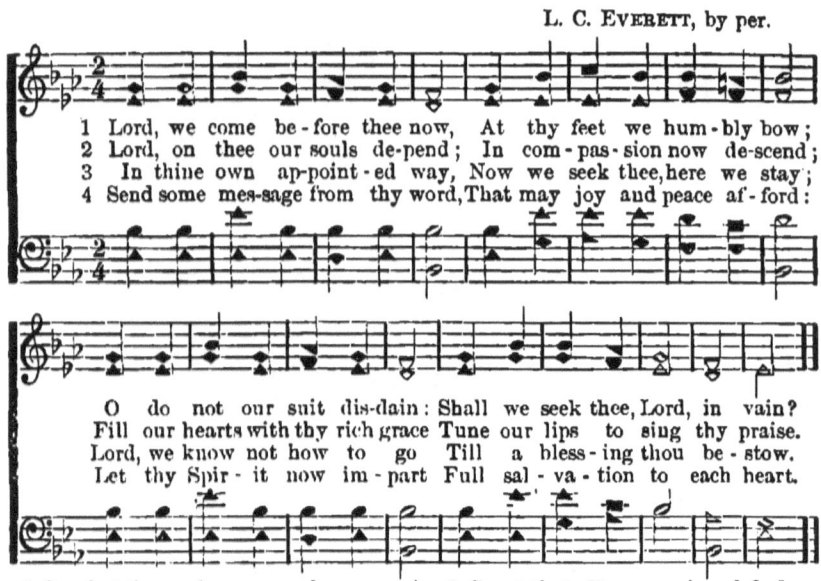

1 Lord, we come before thee now, At thy feet we humbly bow;
2 Lord, on thee our souls depend; In compassion now descend;
3 In thine own appointed way, Now we seek thee, here we stay;
4 Send some message from thy word, That may joy and peace afford:

O do not our suit disdain: Shall we seek thee, Lord, in vain?
Fill our hearts with thy rich grace Tune our lips to sing thy praise.
Lord, we know not how to go Till a blessing thou bestow.
Let thy Spirit now impart Full salvation to each heart.

5 Comfort those who weep and mourn,
Let the time of joy return;
Those that are cast down lift up,
Make them strong in faith and hope.

6 Grant that all may seek and find
Thee a gracious God, and kind;
Heal the sick, the captive free;
Let us all rejoice in thee.

No. 164. REVIVE US.

1 All glory and praise be to Jesus our Lord, So plenteous in
2 To us he hath given the gift from above,—The earnest of
3 Ye all may receive, who on Jesus do call, The gift of his
4 The peace and the power, ye sinners embrace, And look for the

grace, and so true to his word.
heaven, the Spirit of love.
Spirit,—'tis proffered to all.
shower,—the Spirit of grace.

REFRAIN.

Hallelujah! Thine the glory, Halle-

REVIVE US. Concluded.

-lu-jah! A-men. Hal-le-lu-jah! Thine the glo-ry, Re-vive us a-gain.

No. 165.   **HERMON. C. M.**

Rev. JOHN P. MCFERRIN.

1 { How hap-py ev-'ry child of grace Who knows his sins for-given; }
   { This earth, he cries, is not my place, I seek my place in heaven; }
A coun-try far from mor-tal sight;—Yet, O, by faith I see:
The land of rest, the saints' de-light, The heav'n prepared for me.

2 O what a blessed hope is ours!
While here on earth we stay,
We more than taste the heavenly powers,
And antedate that day:
We feel the resurrection near,
Our life in Christ concealed,
And with his glorious presence here
Our earthen vessels filled.

3 O, would he more of heaven bestow,
And let the vessels break,
And let our ransomed spirits go,
To grasp the God we seek;
In rapturous awe on him to gaze,
Who bought the sight for me.
And shout, and wonder at his **grace**,
To all eternity!

No. 166.   GREENVILLE. 8, 7. Double.

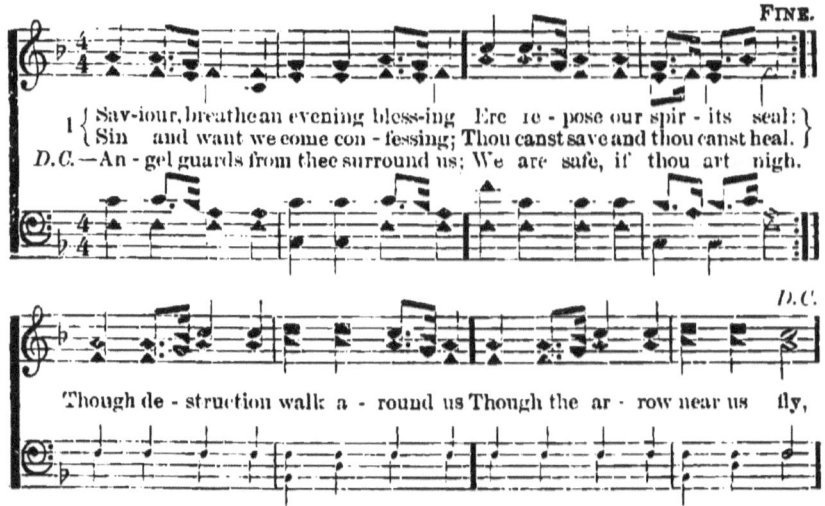

1 { Sav-iour, breathe an evening bless-ing Ere re - pose our spir - its seal; }
  { Sin and want we come con - fessing; Thou canst save and thou canst heal. }
D.C.—An - gel guards from thee surround us; We are safe, if thou art nigh.

Though de - struction walk a - round us Though the ar - row near us fly,

2 Though the night be dark and dreary, | Should swift death this night o'ertake
Darkness cannot hide from thee; | And our couch become our tomb, [us,
Thou art he who, never weary, | May the morn in heaven awake us,
Watcheth where thy people be. | Clad in light, and deathless bloom.

No. 167. 8, 7.

1 Lord, dismiss us with thy blessing, | Fill each breast with consolation:
Bid us now depart in peace; | Up to thee our hearts we raise:
Still on heavenly manna feeding, | When we reach our blissful station,
Let our faith and love increase: | Then we'll give thee nobler praise.

No. 168.   OLD HUNDRED. L. M.

Praise God, from whom all blessing flow; Praise him, all creatures here below;

Praise him above, ye heavenly host; Praise Father, Son, and Ho - ly Ghost.

INDEX OF TITLES AND FIRST LINES.

A

	No.
A charge to keep I have	86
Albion	148
All glory and praise be to Jesus	164
All hail the power of Jesus	109
A loving voice is calling from on	69
Amazing grace, how sweet the sound	21
And can I yet delay	144
Antioch. C. M	44
Are there few that be saved	5
Arlington. C. M	55
As forth from the city went Jesus	14
Ashville. C. M	160
A sinner, I came, for my Lord to see	3
As pants the hart	131
As shadows cast by cloud and sun	38
As we've sown so shall we reap	133
At the sounding of the trumpet	136
At the feast of Belshazzar	103

B

Back from the long ago	135
Beautiful Zion	29
Because He first loved me	129
Behold th' amazing sight	158
Be it my only wisdom	111
Beyond the smiling and the weeping	57
Beyond the sunset	91
Beyond this life of hope and fears	48
Blessed is He	119
Blind Bartimeus	14
Bonnell. C. M	159
Boylston. S. M	130
Bright Jewels	116
Brightly shines redeeming mercy	45
Brightly, sweetly, toiling for thee	11
Bring them in	67
Broker. L. M	141
Brother, look out o'er the	121
By faith we find the place above	122
By their fruits	66

C

Calling for thee	121
Capers. C. M	151

	No.
Children of Jerusalem	79
Christmas Bells	94
Christ, the Lord, is risen to-day!	161
Cleave to the Saviour	137
Come and join our band	95
Come, Holy Spirit, Come	157
Come, sinner, to the gospel feast	143
Come, thou almighty King	148
Come to Jesus right away	10
Come to Jesus, youthful pilgrims	10
Come unto me all ye weary and	68
Come unto me, come unto me	47
Coronation. C. M	109
Crichlow. L. M	155

D

Davies. 7s	72
Daybreak	70
Dear Sabbath home	81
Did Christ o'er sinners weep?	130
Doggett. C. M	138
Do you ask why I love Jesus?	129
Duke Street. L. M	126
Duncan. S. M	162
Drifting toward the golden shore	127

E

Enough for me	65
Ev'ry day brings us nearer to	123

F

Fade, fade each earthly joy	1
Farmville	149
Father, I stretch my hands to Thee	146
Father of mercies	102
Flitting away	33
Follow me	24
For thee, oh! sinless Eden	120
Forever here my rest shall be	151
From every stormy wind that blows	62

G

Gather around the Christmas	112
Georgia. S. M	158
Gill. 8s, 7s, & 4s. (8th P. M.)	154

	No.
Give me thy heart	9
God be with you	78
God is calling you	74
Go gather the golden grain	58
Go through the gates	96
Go to the souls that are lost	77
God wants the boys and girls	110
God wants the boys, the mercy	110
Go wash in the blood	46
Going home	28
Gregory	111
Greenville. 8, 7, Double	166

H

Hallelujah! bless His name	3
Happy day. L. M	107
Handwriting on the wall	103
Hark! a voice from Eden stealing	53
Hark! the Christmas bells are	94
Hark! 'tis the Shepherd's voice I	67
Harp. C. M	21
Have you heard the olden story	9
Have you looked to Jesus for His	46
Head. C. M	156
Hear how a sower once	4
Hear the jubilant song that the	63
Hear the Master calling	56
Hebron. L. M	124
Helen. C. M	153
Hermon. C. M	165
Her sad vigil keeping	2
He's watching o'er me	43
Hide me, O my Saviour, hide me	92
Hide me, Saviour	92
High in the heavens, eternal God	140
Hold my hand	13
Home. C. M., Double	132
Hosanna	83
Hosanna to Jesus, our	83
How happy every child of grace	165
How sweet the name of Jesus sounds	159

I

I am drifting down the stream	127
I am longing for the coming of the	17
I am the light of the world	47

	No.
I am trusting Thee	40
I dare not idle stand	61
I hear a song, a song so sweet	64
In days of old, near Jericho	106
In the shadow of His wings	27
In the vineyard of the Master	49
It is better farther on	53
I know that my Redeemer lives	160
I will lift my voice in a song of	33

J

Jesus! and shall it ever be	155
Jesus, I my cross have taken	34
Jesus is calling for thee	134
Jesus is mighty to save	77
Jesus is mine	1
Jesus is passing to-day	106
Jesus, lover of my soul	128
Jesus, my Lord, to Thee I cry	59
Jesus shall reign where'er the	126
Jesus taught the waiting people	24
Jesus, the Conqu'ror, reigns	147
Jesus, to Thee I now can fly	145
Jesus, wearied with His journey	7
Joyously on	85
Joy to the world, the Lord is	44
Just as I am	149
Just as I am, O Lord, I come to Thee	15

K

Kavanaugh. L. M	143
Kerlin. C. M	152

L

Laban. S. M	113
Lebanon. 7s	161
Lest in weakness I may stray	13
Let every tongue Thy goodness speak	156
Let them come	16
Let us pass over the river	36
Liken the kingdom to the springing	19
Look away to Calv'ry's rugged	8
Lord, dismiss us with Thy blessing	167
Lord, we come before Thee now	163
Loving Jesus, gentle Lamb	72

M

	No.
Marching on an army, strong	85
Martyn. 7s, Double	128
McCoy. S. M	157
Meet me there	97
Messiah comes, the mighty	88
Mighty to save	96
Moulton. S. M	144
My God, the spring of all my joys	153
My house on a rock	52
My soul, be on thy guard	113
My soul repeat His praise	25

N

Nearer home	123
Nearer to Thee	135

O

O happy day that fixed	107
Oh! if my house is built upon a	52
Oh, to be there	71
O land of rest for Thee I	132
O lead me to Jesus	104
O love, surpassing knowledge	65
Onward, upward	115
O the unsearchable riches of Christ	76
O Thou God of my salvation	154
Oh, I love to think how Jesus	16
Old Hundred. L. M	168
Once a feast was made and the	75
Once, forth to meet the	99
Once more we come before our God	55
On the distant heathen shore	39
On the happy golden shore	97
On the mountain's top appearing	105
Over the sea	39

P

Paul. S. M	147
Pilgrim, through this barren land	35
Praise God from whom all blessings	168
Praise the Lord	108
Precious forever, Oh! wonderful	89
Precious words	89
Press onward	73
Pumroy. 7s	163

R

	No.
Radiant clime of the pure	71
Rallying song	95
Redeeming mercy	45
Rejoice in the Lord	23
Repeat the sweet story of Jesus to	41
Revive us	164
Retreat. L. M	62
Richmond. S. M	86
Rock of Ages. 7s, 6 lines	50
Ross. C. M	122

S

Say, are few to be saved of men	5
Saviour, breathe an evening blessing	166
Saviour, wash me	15
Scatter bright smiles	118
Schumann. S. M	150
Send the joyful proclamation	100
Shall we know each other there?	42
Sharing so freely the gifts of the	23
Solitude. C. M	145
Some day	64
Some sweet day	82
Sow in the morn thy seed	162
Spring. C. M	146
St. Thomas. S. M	25
Summers. L. M	140
Sweet rest	68

T

Take me as I am	59
Take my life and let it be	98
Tarry and rest	7
The barren fig-tree	49
The fields are ripe with the harvest	58
The flowing fountain	8
The gates of mercy	37
The home where changes never	117
The hope of the soul	125
The joyful proclamation	100
The Lord is my Shepherd	87
The Lord my Shepherd is	150
The Lord of Sabbath let us praise	138
The lost sheep	12
The marriage of the King's Son	75

	No.
The Master calleth for thee	2
The message of salvation	90
The morning bright, with rosy light	152
The mustard seed	19
The narrow way	93
The ninety and nine, His dear ones	12
The olden story	9
There's a message of salvation	90
There is a Rock in a weary land	30
There was love, deep love, in the	6
The Saviour is watching by night	43
The sheltering Rock	30
The sinless summer land	17
The soul hath a hope ever	125
The sower	4
The sweet story	41
The ten virgins	99
The welcome refrain	63
They say there's a land o'er the	32
This life is a fanciful stage	101
Thus far the Lord hath led	124
The way to Heaven is narrow	93
The land of Calvary	6
'Tis midnight, and on Olive's brow	141
Toiling for Jesus	11
To that "heavenly home" blest	23
Trust Him	35

U

Unsearchable riches	76

V

Virginia. C. M	142
Vaughan. C. M	139

W

Wait and murmur not	117
Walk in the light! and thou shalt	54

	No.
Walk in the marvelous light	54
We are coming	114
We are marching to the kingdom	26
We have heard Thy gentle	114
We'll gather the children of want	51
We'll gather them in	51
We shall be like Him	31
We shall reach the river	82
We silently slumber at last	101
We sing Thy praises, O Zion to-day	29
What a gathering that will be	136
When, as of old, in her sadness	134
When Jesus shall make up His	116
When musing sorrow weeps the	142
When our work is ended, we shall	36
When the clouds have left the	70
When the mists have cleared away	60
When the mists have rolled in	60
When the worn spirit wants repose	139
When we've cross'd death's solemn	42
Where are you going, Oh! sinner	20
Where shall we go?	84
Who, among the mighty?	88
Who'll be leading	18
Will sing with joy	33
Will you be there?	48
Wonderful words for all	80
Wonderful words, God has spoken	80
Working, O Christ, with Thee	23
Working with Thee	22
Would you go with the angels	20
Would you please and honor Jesus	137

Y

Yarbrough	98
You who long in sin have wandered	87

Z

Zion. 8s, 7s and 4s	105

www.ingramcontent.com/pod-product-compliance
Lightning Source LLC
Chambersburg PA
CBHW020251170426
43202CB00008B/321